life and livelihood

A HANDBOOK

FOR SPIRITUALITY

AT WORK

WHITNEY WHERRETT ROBERSON

MOREHOUSE PUBLISHING
A Continuum imprint
HARRISBURG • LONDON • NEW YORK

Except as indicated, all quotations from Scripture are from the New Revised Standard Version Bible, copyright © 1989, Division of Christian Education of the National Council of the Churches of Christ in the United States of America. Used by permission. All rights reserved.

Morehouse Publishing, P.O. Box 1321, Harrisburg, PA 17105
Morehouse Publishing, The Tower Building, 11 York Road, London SE1 7NX
Morehouse Publishing is a Continuum imprint.

Cover design by Corey Kent

Library of Congress Cataloging-in-Publication Data

Roberson, Whitney Wherrett.
    Life and livelihood : a handbook for spirituality at work / Whitney Wherrett Roberson.
        p.   cm.
    Includes bibliographical references.
    ISBN 0-8192-2136-8 (pbk.)
    1. Employees—Religious life.   2. Work—Religious aspects—Christianity.   I. Title.
BV4593.R62   2004
248.8′8—dc22

                                                                            2004006884

Printed in the United States of America

04 05 06 07 08 09   6 5 4 3 2 1

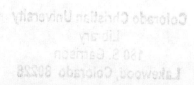

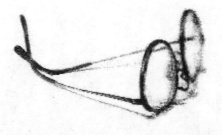

This book is dedicated to my parents, Norm and Lynne Wherrett, whose spirituality has always informed their approach to life and livelihood.

And to John McGuinn and Colby Cogswell whose commitment to the Conversation made Spirituality at Work possible.

contents

Part I: The Basics

Part II: The SAW Agendas

Sample Agendas

Part III: Other Conversation Formats for Spirituality at Work Groups

preface

We'd been sitting around the table for almost an hour, sorting through our frustrations about work: a disappointing lack of trust, uncertain job security coupled with an increasing workload, the longing for greater connection and meaning in our work. "What questions are emerging from our stories?" the conversation facilitator had just wondered to the group. The business professionals fell silent for a moment, reflecting soberly. Then an attorney spoke into the silence, "My question is simple, really: wherein lies our hope?"

Spirituality at Work began as an experiment: a small group of individuals whose spiritual roots lay in the Christian tradition met to explore the relationship between their work and their faith. Facilitated by a graduate student studying theology and transformative learning,[1] the conversations developed into a project to discover how participants might open up "conversation spaces" in which they could help each other integrate the inner life of spirit with the outer life of work. They hoped to deepen their own sense of meaning and purpose, and wondered how they could create "circles of hope," moving themselves, their work, and their workplaces toward a deeper wholeness. The inquiry, begun as a graduate student's independent study course, gathered momentum, resources, and participants, and soon becoming a project of the Episcopal Diocese of California: Spirituality at Work.

Since that first conversation, SAW has evolved into a community concerned with exploring links between what we do, who we are, and what we believe. We've initiated and facilitated conversations in which participants have sought a deeper awareness of the reality of Spirit in their lives. We formed our own organization and received funding to expand our conversations, consulting with individuals and communities and providing resources for their use. We've now moved beyond organization, returning to a less-structured community. We remain committed, however, to offering what we've learned to others who share our vision and who wish to form communities of encouragement and to empower one another as agents of hope in their work.

This book is one such offering. It is intended to provide a starting point for individuals or communities who want to explore spirituality in the context of work. It contains some reflections about our own experience of initiating and supporting generative conversations, along with a sampling—about a year's worth—of the conversation outlines, or "agendas," we've developed to facilitate this sort of conversation. We use the term "agenda" with tongue in cheek: our lives are too often bound by agendas developed for us by others. This book seeks to put something new on the agenda, offering our deepest selves, our souls, a place at the table. This "new agenda" is, we hope, one that we can all truly embrace as our own. We hope you'll feel free to use the conversation agendas as they are, as models for developing other issues or as jumping-off places for generating your own materials. The final section of the book suggests some additional conversation formats we've used and can recommend.

We invite you to get in touch with us through our website (www.spirit uality at work.com) if you have questions, comments, or simply want to share what you're learning. Welcome to the conversation!

Whitney Wherrett Roberson
San Francisco

Note

1. This refers to a kind of adult education that aims at a deeper examination and transformation of one's perspectives and assumptions.

acknowledgments

In a very real sense, this book has been a collaborative process from the start. It was created in the context of Spirituality at Work conversations, the many participants in those conversations helping to generate the questions, insights, and strategies found herein. I acknowledge their contributions with deep gratitude.

In addition, special thanks must go to those who served on the several working teams of Spirituality at Work: especially to Carol Castellini, John McGuinn, and Cal Rutherford who chaired these teams; and to Mary Wagner, Sara Achenbach, Paul Evans, John Castello, Steve White, Lilli Lindbeck, Deborah Fraugquist and Jane Grodem, each of whom offered their unique gifts to the organization, giving hours of their time so the conversation might continue.

Everyone needs "fans," those generous friends of the soul who offer unqualified support when we find ourselves uncertain of our own "next steps." I count among mine Martin Rutte, Bob and Barbara Langbauer, Judith and Jay Rock, Lana Kreivis, Jack Bunzel, and my children and their spouses Rachel and Lori, Rebecca, and Sarah and Michael.

part I:
the basics

soul-making—
moving toward shalom

Not a bible study, a ministry team nor even, in the usual sense of the word, a support group, a spirituality at work conversation group is intended to transform participants, offering them not just the opportunity to connect what they do with what they believe or most value, but a community in which they can explore what it might mean to *act* from such connections. Here are the ways we've come to understand spirituality at work.

Spirituality at work conversations are about soul-making

An ancient spiritual concept, soul-making is making a comeback in both spiritual and psychological circles. Thomas Moore, author of *Care of the Soul,* suggests that the spiritual and psychological belong together, that an inquiry into each is a part of soul-making. Our perspective is that soul-making includes both and more, for the soul, as we understand it, lies at the intersection of our spiritual, emotional, intellectual, social, and physical selves. Soul is fundamentally who we are at the deepest level of our being; it is *all* of who we are. In Moore's words, "soul has to do with genuineness and depth . . . is tied to life in all its particulars . . . is revealed in attachment, love, and community as well as in retreat . . . inner communing and intimacy."[1] If soul-making is about "all of who we are," then

3

it is also about who we are at work, and it is about the communities we form at work and the nature of our work itself. Spirituality at work conversation explores all these areas.

Spirituality at work is about *shalom*

A Hebrew word, *shalom* is often translated as *peace,* and yet its meaning is much richer and more profound. Shalom suggests a wholeness or health and carries with it a sense of fullness, abundance, completeness in a larger Reality. Shalom doesn't necessarily mean everything is rosy or calm, but it *does* suggest a confidence that, in this larger Reality all will be well. Shalom is about the generous hospitality of divine Mystery, about the willingness of this Mystery to make a place where we can "live and move and have our being," a place to which we can bring *all* of ourselves. Even our unlovely and troublesome bits are part of our wholeness and, within the love of the divine Reality, are woven into the fabric of our being, becoming creative and life-giving. So then, even times of turmoil can be creative when they are understood as part of a larger shalom.

Spirituality at work is about abundant life

It is not first and foremost about achieving our goals, making more money, becoming better managers, finding ways to get others to do what we want, or even about becoming happier, although any and all of these may and do happen when soul-making is taken seriously. What spirituality at work *is* about is abundant life: living fully into each moment, paying attention to what's happening within us and around us, understanding what our lives are about and how we're meant to make a difference within the larger communities of which we are a part. It is, finally, about our deciding to act, to make creative choices that will move us and our organizations toward a deeper wholeness.

Exploring Basic Assumptions

Those of us who began Spirituality at Work held some basic assumptions, and it seems important to be straightforward in sharing these with you. You need not agree with these in order to engage in meaningful conversation about spirituality at work. But we suggest it would be useful for you to discover and examine the assumptions you *do* hold about what's real, since these will surely affect your participation in the conversation, whether as convenor or participant.

Based on our experience, here is what we assume about Who and What Is:

- Divine Mystery or Spirit is real and supports life and wholeness. We want to affirm our experience of the reality of the Divine without narrower definition. Most spiritual traditions agree that the Divine is simply too big for our language; *divine Mystery* is an expression that acknowledges this while still affirming a greater and deeper Reality.
- Human beings—and all of creation—are invited to participate in the life-giving wholeness of the Divine.
- Divine Mystery is present everywhere: at work, at home, within each of us. When we listen with care to one another and pay attention to what's happening around us, we may catch glimpses of this Reality and hear Spirit inviting us to experience, share, and manifest shalom.
- Divine Mystery is not "tame." Reality cannot be manipulated for our own ends, although all of us are invited to facilitate the life-giving hospitality of this Mystery.
- Spiritual wisdom is available to all who seek it. This wisdom is the gift of divine Mystery and is not the exclusive "property" of any religious tradition. Nor is it a function of academic knowledge or training; one need not be an "expert" to access it. Rather, such wisdom is available to everyone who genuinely seeks it.

But what does all this *mean;* and how on earth are we to *do* spirituality at work—soul-making? These are the very questions we ask in our spirituality at work communities, and we've discovered there are no "right answers." What it means to live abundantly or to facilitate wholeness in today's workplaces is something for the people in those workplaces to discover. Will it mean talking about divine Mystery or spiritual things at work? For a few, maybe; for most, probably not. Will it mean learning how to be a reconciling presence at work? Very likely. Will it mean discovering the deeper meaning of our work? Probably. Will it mean fostering the spiritual questing of those closest to us at work? For some, yes. Will it mean building community or imagining ways to effect systemic change or institutional transformation at work? Yes, it might.

It might mean all or any of these, as well as many other possibilities. But what's most important for now is that we don't have to explore the questions alone! Together, as we talk and support one another, we gradually discern the appropriate ways each of us can become shalom-bearing agents of transformation and reconciliation within our life and work contexts.

starting a conversation

The Place to Start: Conversation Becoming Community

Spirituality at work conversation is about creating a safe place to talk about the things that matter most to us and about connecting these things to our daily lives and work. Those who convene SAW groups create "conversation spaces," helping to move participants toward a creative community in which they are encouraged both to support one another and to bring their experience and wisdom to bear on the challenging questions of the contemporary workplace. Actually, most of us create "conversation spaces" all the time without much thought. Initiating spirituality at work conversation simply requires us to be a little more intentional about the process.

So how do you get a conversation started? Try these steps.

Step One: Find allies—one or two others who might share your interest in spirituality at work

- If you have a faith community, this is one place to start. Discover whether other members of your community work near you or do the same kind of work you do by checking with the leadership of your faith community, posting a notice on a bulletin board or in a newsletter, or making an announcement at a community gathering. If you don't have a faith community, look to your workplace or professional community as a source for allies. Pay attention at work or professional gatherings; you may notice someone whose comments or questions suggest an openness to spirituality at work conversation.

■ Meet once or twice informally with your potential allies to investigate the possibility of hosting an exploratory meeting with a larger group. Discuss who else in your faith community, organization, or work neighborhood might be interested in issues related to spirituality at work.

Step Two: With your allies, host an exploratory meeting

■ Invite potential participants to meet for lunch or after work near your workplace or in your home. Personal invitations often work best initially: either chat with people directly or send a note or memo. In some contexts, a more public announcement might be appropriate.

■ At this meeting, share your own interest in spirituality at work and why you feel an ongoing conversation would be helpful. Invite others to do the same. A sample agenda for an exploratory meeting is included in this handbook (see One Exploratory Meeting Agenda on page 10).

■ Suggest participants share the issues they might want to discuss. One way to approach this is to ask people to share their frustrations and satisfactions about work: where are they passionate about their work and where do they experience pain at work? Make a list of these and of any questions that emerge from these "pains and passions." Each question or issue is a potential focus for a conversation.

■ Discuss the concerns the group has about starting such a conversation. Some common concerns include:

✔ *Time commitment:* People are often concerned about making a long-term commitment to attend meetings. One solution is to ask for a very limited initial commitment—say three or four sessions—so that participants can get to know one another a bit. After this brief initial commitment, members can feel free to come whenever they're able.

✔ *Frequency of meetings:* Busy work or family schedules make it difficult for most people to attend weekly meetings. But when groups meet less frequently, participants lose track of the meeting times. A good compromise is to agree to meet weekly for a month or six weeks and then re-evaluate, perhaps moving to a twice-a-month or monthly meeting.

✓ *Length and time of meetings:* Meetings of one hour right before work or at lunch seem to work for many people. If the group decides to meet less often than once a week, one and a half or two hours may work better. It's important to honor agreements about time, however; potential participants need to know that if the group agrees to meet for just an hour, it will be just an hour.

✓ *Conversation format:* A simple format that you use every time may work best. A year's worth of SAW conversation agendas are included in this book. A number of alternative formats are also outlined.

✓ *Leadership:* Although most groups have one or two convenors (perhaps you and your allies) who initiate the conversation and take some responsibility for disseminating information about the group's life, *all* participants can take a turn facilitating the conversation, using the simple materials provided in this book. Rotating leadership means that no one, not even the convenors, must attend every time.

✓ *Meeting site:* Public restaurants work fine for spirituality at work conversations, although they can be noisy and ordering can take time away from the conversation. A company cafeteria can work well since participants can get a meal quickly or even bring their own food. An office or conference room is a nice alternative, if available and easily accessible; participants can bring their own food.

■ Be prepared to continue the exploratory conversation into a second meeting if potential participants need more time to lay the foundation for an ongoing conversation. It's important to honor any time limits you've set for this first meeting.

■ Before adjourning, agree to any "next steps" you and the others might take to move the group closer to setting up the ongoing conversation.

Step Three: Begin the conversation

■ Read over the facilitation tips beginning on page 21. As other participants take their turn at facilitating, encourage them to look them over as well.

■ Take some time early in the group's life to talk about conversation ground rules, such as the importance of respecting confidentiality and encouraging all points of view (see Typical Conversation Norms or Ground Rules on page 11).

■ The principal convenors will probably assume facilitation responsibilities for the group for the first few meetings, modeling the sort of facilitation you hope will become the norm for the group. Then set up a facilitation schedule in conversation with the other participants.

One Exploratory Meeting Agenda (1 to 1½ Hours)

Gathering (5 to 10 minutes)

- Name tags are a good idea, as all participants may not be acquainted.
- Be sure to have a sign-in sheet, on which attendees list their names and contact information.
- If the gathering is not at a mealtime, plan to have some food appropriate for the time of day. (Keep in mind: some folks don't eat sweets and some avoid animal foods, so have a variety of goodies available.)
- As convenor(s) you will want to be sure to welcome people warmly, especially those who might not know others at the gathering.

Welcome and greeting (5 to 10 minutes)

- Each of you convening the gathering will want to introduce yourself, telling folks your name, where you work or the kind of work you do, and briefly why you're interested in spirituality at work and why you initiated the gathering. (If appropriate, you may also want to include your faith community or spiritual tradition/background as part of your introduction.)
- Review the agenda with the group, asking for comments, additions, and so on. Most folks will be amenable, but it's useful to set a collaborative tone even at this first meeting.

Introductions (1 or 2 minutes per person)

- If there are more than 10 people, divide into groups of no more than 6 each.
- Invite others to introduce themselves in the way you've just modeled, that is, to say: a) their name; b) where they work or the kind of work they do; c) if they wish, their spiritual tradition/background; and d) why they accepted the invitation to come to the meeting.

Sharing our experiences of work (2 to 4 minutes per person, but no more than 25 minutes total)

- Again, if the group is larger than 10 people, divide into small groups.
- Invite people to share their greatest frustrations about their work or workplace (about 10 minutes).
  - ✔ You may want to give folks a chance to reflect privately on this for a moment, providing paper and pencils to jot down their thoughts before they share aloud.
  - ✔ As people share, write their frustrations on a flip chart.

- Ask participants to share satisfactions about work, and note these on the flip chart (about 10 minutes).
- Ask whether the group can re-frame their satisfactions and frustrations in the form of questions; as they review the lists, do any "burning questions" emerge? For example, the frustration with a workplace culture where everyone is too busy to interact much with colleagues becomes a question about "How can I create community at work?"
- Comment that the lists the group has generated might become the basis for a series on ongoing conversations and see whether there's interest in continuing this sort of conversation.

Planning next steps (10 to 15 minutes)
- If some of the participants are interested in continuing the conversation, discuss their concerns and decide when and where to meet again.
- One of the convenors should take responsibility for contacting those interested in continuing. (Personal follow-up and reminders are crucial to getting a group off the ground!)

Closing (5 minutes)
- Invite participants to share one or two words expressing their hope for the group. It's often helpful to have one of the convenors begin, thus modeling the process for the others.
- And/or invite each person to offer the person on his/her left a personal word of hope for the coming week. Again, the facilitator begins.

Typical Conversation Norms or "Ground Rules"

Sometime early in the life of a conversation group, participants usually find it helpful to talk about the conversation norms or ground rules it wants to set for itself. As an articulation of the values that form and inform a particular conversation community, the ground rules may vary from group to group. But we've found a few that seem especially to support our conversations.

Confidentiality
Spirituality at work conversations are intended to be safe spaces in which participants can open up to one another and to divine Mystery as

they explore matters they value deeply. The assurance that what is said will remain private is one way to create such a safe space.

Honoring all perspectives

One of our primary assumptions is that Spirit-inspired wisdom will emerge from the group as each participant shares his/her own lived experiences, honest perspectives, and heart-felt questions. Consequently, all perspectives are heard with respect and honored. When tension between the perspectives of participants arises, this tension is held lightly within the generous and hospitable context of the conversation. Participants learn to trust that wisdom is often born in and from such tension and that Spirit often speaks from the paradox of apparent opposites.

Speaking authentically

A part of honoring all perspectives is honoring one's own and speaking authentically from one's own truth, taking full "ownership" of what one sees, feels, and believes. We claim and speak from our own understanding, even as we leave others free to do the same. We're not trying to change minds or hearts here, but rather hoping to open minds and hearts more deeply, beginning with our own!

Paraphrasing

The process just described necessitates a deep understanding of both self and other. We encourage participants to seek this deeper understanding by paraphrasing another's perspective before responding directly to it, especially when there is any danger of misunderstanding. Giving the other a chance to be heard deeply contributes both to a mutual and profound understanding and to a fuller level of trust within the group. Paraphrasing is one way to demonstrate that the listener has truly heard what the speaker intended. Further, it gives the speaker a chance to clarify or refine anything that has not been completely understood.

Respecting time norms

Since many spirituality at work conversations are held before or during the work day, it is essential to honor the time norms the group sets for itself. When participants know they will not be "trapped" in a conversation that intrudes on their workday and that the facilitator will keep track of the time, they are more likely to enter fully into the conversation and return another time.

At each conversation, the facilitator holds for the group these norms—and any others the group sets for itself—supporting participants as they seek to honor the norms. Some groups print their norms on a chart or on small cards that are displayed in some way during the conversation. Honoring such norms is a way participants honor one another. Groups that respect their own values move more rapidly toward real community.

Legal Issues Convenors Should Know

Lilli Lindbeck is an employment law attorney who worked as an intern with Spirituality at Work. She prepared these notes regarding legal issues that might pertain to SAW conversations. If you have other questions or concerns about such legal issues, please contact Spirituality at Work through our website, and we will put you in touch with Lilli directly.

If your SAW group includes more than one person from the same workplace, or if you are interested in approaching your employer for permission to hold an SAW conversation at a particular location, it is important that you be aware of the legal rules governing religion in the workplace.

- Federal (and state) equal employment law prohibits employers from discriminating on the basis of religion in the workplace. Federal law defines *religion* as including "all aspects of religious observance and practice as well as belief." Federal law defines *discrimination* broadly; employers may not impose religion as a condition of employment nor may employers condone an atmosphere of religious harassment (e.g., threats, humiliation, persuasion, and offensive comments).
- SAW conversations are strictly voluntary and encourage the sharing of beliefs in an atmosphere of shalom in which all perspectives are honored. Agendas for SAW conversations demonstrate hospitality to anyone interested in soul-making, regardless of faith tradition. SAW conversations neither impose a religion on participants nor do they condone harassment. Therefore, equal employment law provisions do not prohibit holding SAW conversations in the workplace.
- Convenors should repeat the principle of shalom and the ground rule of honoring all perspectives whenever an SAW group begins, new participants join the conversation, or any concern arises about the imposition of religion or harassment within the group (see Typical Conversation Norms or Ground Rules).
- Federal and state employment laws require the accommodation of religious "observance and practice as well as belief," except where the employer is unable to reasonably accommodate such observance or practice without undue hardship on the conduct of the employer's business. An SAW conversation is not a religious observance or prac-

tice, so employers are not *required* to permit such conversations on their premises or give extra time off for such conversations.
- Finally, some employers bar solicitation at work. SAW conversations, typically, do not involve fundraising, dues, or membership. Thus solicitation rules do not affect SAW conversations.

Since the law is neutral on holding SAW conversations in the workplace, the location of your SAW group is a matter of choice. If your employer has questions, you may wish to show him/her this book and/or extend an invitation to your first meeting.

Facilitating a Conversation: Some Basics

Participants in SAW conversations are both facilitators and participants. As facilitators, we help other participants share their thoughts/feelings and support one another, *and* we contribute our own thoughts/feelings to the conversation. If you find it difficult to do both initially, you can focus solely on being facilitator. Here are some simple ways to do this. (For more detailed facilitation tips, see "Facilitation Tips" on page 21.)

Before each session
Preparation need take only about 10 minutes.
- Hold group members in your heart and mind even though you may not know exactly who will show up. Imagine the group becoming a community of hope and compassion.
- Reread the conversation agenda you've chosen or prepared.
- Review the facilitation tips on page 21.

As you facilitate
The principal task of the SAW facilitator is to guide the group to reflect and share wisdom by encouraging members to support one another as they focus on a common concern or question.
- Trust the Spirit: In the final analysis, SAW conversations are not ours but part of a bigger Reality.
- Trust yourself: Be authentic and explore the truth of your own experience. In this way you are modeling appropriate vulnerability for the rest of the group.
- Know that you do not need to have answers: *Facilitating* doesn't mean teaching or even leading. Your job is to help the group listen to itself and to the Divine in one another.

■ Honor all perspectives, and be open to surprise: Spirit shows up in unexpected ways!
■ Do it with love.
■ Ask for wisdom, patience, and "ears to hear."

After the session

A facilitator can continue to be an effective community builder even after the conversation.

■ Acknowledge privately anyone whose contribution was especially helpful to you, who is experiencing a lot of stress at the moment, or who seems unsettled by the conversation. This acknowledgment may necessitate a phone call. Trust your instincts: if it seems important to follow up with someone, do so.
■ Continue to hold a good thought for everyone in the group.

Convenor Tips: Keeping the Conversation Community Vital

Although the facilitator's role may rotate among members, it's important for the group to have one or two designated convenors. Often, though not necessarily, the co-convenors called the group into being in the first place. They are the principal "agents of hospitality" for the group, maintaining personal contact with participants and fostering connections within the group.

Here are a few things we've noticed that most effective convenors do to maintain a strong, ongoing conversation community:

Maintain general oversight

Someone needs to take responsibility for the "nuts and bolts" issues of the group: maintaining and communicating the facilitator schedule, making sure facilitators have the materials they need and are ready when it's their turn to facilitate, negotiating site changes if they become necessary, and generally overseeing the life of the conversation community as it develops.

Communicate regularly

Successful convenors keep in touch with participants, reminding them of meeting times and inviting their regular participation. Sometimes e-mail or postcards do the trick, but personal communication of some sort often seems to be important. Reminders that invite rather than coerce seem to work best. Participants appreciate knowing that their contributions to the conversation are valued and that they're missed when they can't make it. On the other hand, they also need to know that when they can't attend for any reason, that's okay and that they're welcome whenever they can rejoin the group.

Offer appropriate personal support

Convenors are well positioned to show ongoing support and concern for individual participants. Occasionally, a participant may be dealing with a troubling life or work issue that invites more than a casual expression of concern. While most SAW convenors are not trained therapists and should not attempt a therapeutic intervention, a phone call or note to a struggling member of the conversation community is almost always appropriate and appreciated. Such a personal response encourages genuine care-taking within the group and fosters a deeper level of community. Making and facilitating real emotional connections with and among participants is clearly one of the most powerful ways to create and maintain this deeper community.

Hold the group in your heart through prayer/meditation

One of the basic assumptions of spirituality at work conversation affirms the presence of the Divine in all times and places. This assumption is supported by our observation that when convenors incorporate concern for their group into their personal spiritual practice, it has a powerful effect on the life of the conversation community and its members. It's as though, by holding the group in his/her heart, the convenor becomes a channel for divine Hospitality.

part II:
the SAW agendas

about the agendas

What follows are ten series of participant agendas or conversation guides for spirituality at work conversation. Each series contains four conversations around a general theme; each conversation within the set focuses on some aspect of this theme. The conversations in each series are designed to be used consecutively over a month or two of meetings, although in most of the series the content of each agenda is self-contained and does not depend for its effectiveness on the material that comes before or after it.

The themes and topics themselves were generated by participants in our SAW groups, so it's hoped they will engender fruitful conversation for those in similar work contexts. While the agendas were developed primarily for business professionals, we imagine many of the themes will be relevant for the wider working community. In any case, we trust you will develop your own agenda around themes that are appropriate for your own group. We hope these materials can serve as a useful model for you. Let us know if we can be helpful to you as you create your own.

Note: Although the agendas are not identical, certain topics appear in more than one agenda series. We've found that many spirituality at work issues are interrelated and that participants often find it useful to consider these issues from several angles. Should a given agenda seem repetitious to members of your group, however, simply substitute a topic of greater relevance to them.

facilitation tips

Using the Conversation Agenda

The basic "agenda" we use for most SAW conversations was developed as a way to move a group into significant conversation quickly. It was designed to make the most of a short conversation by focusing and maintaining the group's attention on a given topic. Intended to facilitate communal reflection on a topic, each agenda should be used in whatever way is genuinely useful to the group: use all or part, adding or skipping questions or even whole sections to meet the needs of your group.

What follows are some general comments and facilitation tips[1] about the various sections of the agenda. For the most part, each agenda begins with a centering experience (Center) intended to remind participants of divine Hospitality that is the context for all spirituality at work conversations. The Check-in that follows reconnects group members and helps participants become fully present to one another. The Focus section introduces the topic of the conversation and gives participants a chance to share something of their own experience in relation to it. A period of communal reflection (Reflect and Connect) follows in which participants are invited to go a little deeper, often by considering one or more perspectives on the topic taken from contemporary or traditional spiritual wisdom, placing these into dialogue with participants' own experience and deriving insights from this dialogue. The final movement of the conversation (Respond) invites participants to consider appropriate action steps they might take in response to the day's discussion, steps that encourage experimenting with new ways of being, doing, and creating in the workplace. A brief ritual of blessing (Bless) closes the group.

Let's look a little more closely at facilitating:

Center

Purpose

- Recall the presence of the Divine.
- Slow down.
- Listen to body, soul, heart.

Facilitation tips

- *Be mindful of the pace.* The tendency is to rush.
- *Use your watch* if it's helpful.
- *Make sure you are centering* even as you encourage others to center.
- *Be aware of tension in your own body* and relax it.

Check in

Purpose

- Help the group become present to one another and to the conversation.
- Help participants talk about and then let go of anything they've brought with them that might make it hard for them to be fully present.
- Allow participants the chance to share the progress—or lack thereof—they've made on an "action step" they've generated for themselves as part of their response to an earlier discussion.

Facilitation tips

- *Encourage brief check-ins.* Check-ins can take over the conversation. Unless the group has decided it wants this, it's better to keep each check-in brief.
- *Discourage "crosstalk."* Invite participants to listen to one another but not comment on another's check-in.
- *Allow non-participation.* Make it clear that passing is okay.
- *Trust your intuition.* If you sense that someone's need to talk during check-in is going to be problematic for the group, acknowledge

his/her sharing and express the hope that the day's conversation will be helpful; if you sense that the group ought to stop and deal with the issue being shared, go with it.

Focus

Purpose
- Introduce the conversation theme and pose questions.
- Invite sharing from participants' own experience.

Facilitation tips
- *Begin by reading* or summarizing (or asking another to read) the Focus introduction and questions that follow.
- *Invite response* with phrases like: "Who would like to begin?" "Anyone willing to tackle one of the questions?" "Which of the questions seems most compelling?"
- *Allow pauses.* Participants may need a chance to reflect on the questions for a moment before responding.
- *Be flexible about the questions.* There's no need for everyone to respond to every question, to take them sequentially, or to discuss all of them. Some questions may be more generative for a group than others; if no one has a comment on one of them, move on.
- *Encourage personal sharing.* Especially in this section encourage participants to share their own memories, anecdotes, and stories. If someone makes a general statement, invite personal sharing by saying something like, "Sue, can you give us a 'for instance' of that from you own experience?" or "Bob, that's an intriguing observation; can you say a little more about how that's worked in your own experience?"
- *Acknowledge contributions.* Acknowledging personal sharing validates the sharer and encourages openness. Keep it fairly simple: "Thanks, Jo" or "Thanks for your willingness to share that" or "We appreciate your openness."
- *Discourage arguing or debating.* In this section, especially, people are sharing experiences that are their own and not open to question; encourage participants to listen to each other without questioning, giving advice, or arguing with another's experience.
- *Invite quiet people into the conversation.* You can offer quiet people the chance to participate by saying things like, "Tim, you seem thoughtful today; do you want to jump in here?" or "Barb, did you want to add anything?"

■ *But don't push.* If someone prefers not to share, accept that gra-
ciously and move on.

Reflect and Connect

Purpose
■ Encourage participants to examine more fully their own understanding of their experience and/or the assumptions underlying
their perspective on the day's topic.
■ Invite participants to reflect more deeply on the topic by a) considering the wisdom of various spiritual traditions, b) putting this
wisdom into conversation with their own perspectives and experience, and c) exploring the connections and insights emerging from
this dialogue.

Facilitation tips
Most of the tips suggested for the Focus section also apply here. In
addition, consider these:
■ *Facilitate, but don't feel you have to teach.* If someone is looking to
you for answers, turn the question back to the person or the whole
group: "That's a great question; what's your sense about it?" or "I'm
not sure; what do the rest of you think?" or "I'm still working on
that one myself; I'd love to hear what others think." Feel free to
comment at some point, but it's probably best to avoid having the
first or last word.
■ *Model openness to all perspectives.* The facilitator's job is to help participants think deeply about the topic. By being open to all perspectives she or he helps create a safe climate in which all can be heard,
in which new perspectives can be explored, and honest thoughts
and feelings shared. An open climate is likely to be most creative for
participants.
■ *Encourage full participation.* Especially if a few are tending to domi-
nate the conversation, invite others in by saying things like, "Ted and
Bill have a lot of ideas about this one; are there other perspectives on
this?" or " Does anyone have an illustration of what Ted and Bill
have been talking about?" or "I wonder if anyone else has a thought
about this question?"
■ *Balance the conversation.* By inviting a variety of perspectives, the
facilitator helps create a climate in which all points of view are welcome. When one or two people are expressing strong conviction
about a topic, you might wonder aloud, "Are there other ways of
looking at this?" or "Has anyone had a different sort of experience?"

- *Hold others back, if necessary.* Sometimes participants get so involved in the conversation that they unwittingly make it difficult for others to join in. Facilitators can gently encourage all to participate by saying things like, "Hold on a sec, Ted, I think Tom wants to get in here . . ." or "Whoa, let's go one at a time; Mary, you first, then Ted . . .".
- *Draw people out when appropriate.* Drawing people out helps them to clarify their thoughts and go deeper into the topic; it also communicates that their thoughts are valued. Draw people out by saying things like, "Can you say a little more about that?" "Could you share an example from your own experience?" "That's fascinating, but I'm not sure I understand exactly what you mean by . . .".
- *Again, allow pauses.* Sometimes a group falls silent for a moment. Perhaps participants are reflecting on the last remark made or on where to go next; maybe someone's preparing to share something deeply felt. The facilitator can help by staying comfortably and attentively present to the group. Trust your intuition: if you sense it's really time for the group to move on, do so; if you sense there's a comment waiting to be said, stay with it.
- *Keep track of time, and signal when it's almost time to move on.* There is almost always more to say about any given topic than the hour will allow. Again, it's crucial that the time norms for SAW conversations be strictly honored, since people have to get back to work or return to their other obligations. If folks feel trapped in a conversation once, they're less likely to return. When you see the time is running on, say something like, "We've got about three more minutes before we need to move on."

Respond

Purpose
- Invite active response to the insights of the conversation.
- Apply the "talk" to the "walk," by suggesting participants generate appropriate "action steps" with which they'll experiment at work in the coming weeks.

Facilitation tips
- *Allow time for this step of the agenda.* It's possible to get so wrapped up in the conversation that the time slips by; and yet if any real transformation is going to take place, it will happen because we seek to be intentional about "walking our talk." Try to allow about five to ten minutes for this step, depending on the number in the group.

- *Model making a decision.* Think about your own action step ahead of time and share it with the group. (Of course, in light of the conversation, you may change your mind, but do be ready to make some public decision.) If action steps are suggested in the agenda, choose one of these or generate your own and share it with the others.
- *Acknowledge reluctance.* If the group seems reluctant to decide on action steps, acknowledge this and invite comment about what's happening: "We seem a little reluctant to move ahead with action steps; I wonder what's holding us back?"
- *Encourage but don't coerce.* SAW conversations are about invitation and hospitality, not coercion or pressuring. If some in the group simply aren't ready to decide on an action step, invite them to continue reflecting on possibilities and suggest that a useful action step may occur to them later.

Bless

Purpose
- Provide an appropriate moment of closure for the group as a whole.
- Send each participant back to his/her workweek with a personal expression of thanks and blessing.
- End as the group began with a reminder of the ongoing presence of divine Mystery at work and in individual lives.

Facilitation tips
- *Allow enough time for this.* Five minutes is about right, more if the group is larger than eight people.
- *Invite participants to offer aloud to the person on their left a personal word of hope or blessing for the coming week.* Often the blessing is more than one word, but almost everyone can offer one word without feeling overwhelmed.
- *Model the ritual by starting yourself.* Begin by offering your blessing to the person on your left, perhaps referring to something this person said in their check-in. "Susan, my word for you is patience: may you have lots of it as you deal with your difficult colleague."
- *Close by thanking the group for coming.* Encourage them to return next time.
- *Note:* If you need to attend to any housekeeping matters, do it quickly at this time.

Some concluding thoughts: SAW conversations are meant to invite the first word, not to be the last word on a given topic. Facilitators do well to remind themselves (and the group) that there's no need to reach consensus, agreement, or even closure at the end of a conversation. Our intention is to begin a conversation that will then continue during the week in the hearts and minds of participants. Whenever participants leave the conversation energized and eager for more, you can be sure divine Hospitality has been at work!

Three Facilitation Challenges

Moving the conversation along/making transitions

To move through an agenda, the facilitator needs to be familiar enough with what's coming to be able to spot an appropriate segue. You can also watch for pauses or other indications that the group is ready to move on. Sometimes the conversation seems to get stuck in one section, and moving on to the next section may provide a way to get unstuck. If no segue or pause presents itself conveniently, you may simply want to say something like, "I wonder if we're ready to move on?" Also, when a certain section of the agenda is proving really generative for the group, you can simply stay with that section, skipping another for that conversation. Whenever possible, though, try to save time for the Respond section.

Handling talkative or needful people

Occasionally, someone will have an urgent concern or need to talk more than usual; something traumatic may have happened at work or an ongoing issue may be consuming the person's attention. And, of course, some folks are just talkers. The "just talkers" can mostly be handled by using the facilitation tips already presented. The needful people, however, may need some special attention. Here are some ways to handle needful people:

- If it's a personal work-related concern or situation, plan a conversation in which you focus exclusively on that person's need. (Case study formats work well for this sort of conversation. See "Part III: Other Conversation Formats for Spirituality at Work Groups" on page 129.)
- If it's an idea or issue that has captured the person, acknowledge its importance and suggest that the group give it the attention it deserves by making it the exclusive focus of an upcoming conversation.
- On rare occasions, you may sense the issue needs to be dealt with immediately. If so, ask whether the group would be willing to focus the conversation on supporting the needful person.

- Some folks may need more care than you and the group are really competent to give; privately, you might encourage the person to seek the help of a professional counselor or consultant.

Minding the time

Since ending on time *is* so important for busy working people, it's incumbent upon the facilitator to mind the time carefully. The facilitation tips suggest ways to move through the conversation. Occasionally, there may be folks who find it very difficult to let go of the conversation. In such cases, insist with good humor that this conversation must end, but suggest that those who wish to may remain at the table after the closing. You may wish to phone these folks later to apologize for having to cut them off and to acknowledge their contribution to the conversation. If it seems wise, you may also want to suggest that the whole group return to the topic another time.

Note

1. Many of the facilitation tips in this section are based on material from Sam Kaner's *Facilitator's Guide to Participatory Decision-Making* (Gabriola Island, BC: New Society Publishers, 1996).

understanding workplace culture[1]

I: *How does it shape us? How can we shape it?*

Center: Reflect for a moment on your last few days at work, picturing any high or low moments. As you breathe in and out, release these moments or situations to divine Mystery. Breathe out any tension you feel with the word *release*. Breathe in deep peace with the word *peace*. Repeat as your breathe: *release . . . peace . . . release . . . peace.*

Check in: Can you share your progress on a recent action step you've generated for yourself? Or, if you prefer, share something about a work-related concern.

Focus: Today we begin a series of conversations exploring the nature and values of our own workplace "cultures" or that of our professions, seeking a deeper awareness of how we both influence and are influenced by these cultures. Let's begin by looking at our own workplaces or professions.

■ In some spiritual traditions, an individual selects or receives an animal that symbolizes his/her nature; what animal would you use

to symbolize your experience of your own profession or work-place? Why?
- What three words would you use to describe the principal values of your workplace or profession?
- Are the values actually practiced different than the stated values of your workplace or profession?

Reflect: Often the "cultural values" of our work or workplace influence us in subtle ways. Becoming more aware of these influences can free us to choose when we will support these values and when we will offer an alternative. Alternative perspectives can actually contribute to the health of an organization, providing it with more options and encouraging creative solutions not yet envisioned.
- How has your workplace or profession "shaped" you since you began your work?
- Have you noticed that things once very important to you are less so now?
- How have you shaped—or *could* you shape—your workplace culture?
- In general, does your workplace encourage, tolerate, or discourage diverse and individual perspectives? How?

Connect: Great spiritual leaders often challenge the prevailing norms of their cultures, calling into question practices that are life-draining. Jesus, for example, suggested that the concern with ritual purity in his own culture was actually inhibiting the very thing it was meant to facilitate, namely, a right relationship with God. Looking at your own workplace or professional practices:
- Do some practices actually inhibit the very thing they are intended to facilitate?
- Are there ways in which you have to leave the "real you" at home when you go to work? Are there ways in which you feel more "real" at work?
- How do the values or norms of your workplace support or hinder your most creative work?
- Are there ways in which the values of your workplace or profession run counter to your own values or the values of your spiritual tradition?

Respond: In subsequent sessions in this series, we will begin looking at the ways values are communicated in our workplace cultures or professions. It might be useful to pay special attention to some attitudes and aspects of our workplaces or professions. For example, you might notice:

- Attitudes toward time and the use of time, and how values about time are communicated.
- How space is allocated and what values this allocation suggests.
- The way language signals what is valued and what is unimportant in your workplace or profession.
- How else might you discover the values alive in your workplace/professional "culture?"

Bless: As we prepare to return to work or other obligations, offer the person on your left a one- or two-word blessing.

Note

1. The inspiration for this agenda series came from *Transforming the People of God* by Denham Grierson (Melbourne, Australia: The Joint Board of Christian Education, 1984).

II: Time and space

Center: Reflect for a moment on your last few days at work, picturing any high or low moments. As you breathe in and out, release these moments or situations to divine Mystery. Breathe out any tension you feel with the word *release*. Breathe in deep peace with the word *peace*. Repeat as your breathe: *release . . . peace . . . release . . . peace.*

Check in: Can you share something of a recent action step you've chosen for yourself? Or, if you prefer, share what has been most life-giving or life-draining about your work week so far.

Focus: Many of the world's great spiritual traditions recognize that human beings are intended to be co-creators with the Divine: not simply part of creation but *agents* of creation; not just shaped *by* our environments but also shapers *of* them. Finding the openings for transformation within our work contexts involves first naming those contexts, noticing what is currently true within them, either for good or ill, and where they may be poised for creative change. Today we pay special attention to two ways we often define our contexts and ourselves within those contexts: time and space. Let's begin by remembering something of our personal histories around time and space.

- Can you remember sayings or family proverbs regarding the use of time or space?

- What were the "special times" of your childhood or youth?
- Did you have a sacred space as a child? What were the sacred spaces of your family or community?

Reflect: Let's turn now to our experience of time and space as we experience it in our professions or work communities. Take a moment to reflect on these questions, jotting down your thoughts if you wish.

Time
- What is the prevailing sense of time in your profession or work community?
- What uses of time are most/least valued or taboo?
- How is your own experience of time shaped by the values of your profession or workplace?
- Are there ways you'd like to step aside from these professional "rules" concerning time?

Space
- What are the "sacred" spaces in your workplace?
- How does allocation of space communicate the values of your workplace or profession?
- What is your experience of space at work?
- How is this experience shaped by the attitudes you notice in your profession/workplace?
- How would changing space communicate a change of perspective?

Connect: Many spiritual traditions suggest that time and space are contained in a greater Reality. Some Western traditions articulate this with prayers like, "O God, our times are in your hand" (The Episcopal Book of Common Prayer) or "The earth is the Lord's and all that is therein" (Hebrew Bible). Such prayers invite us to see our own attitudes toward time and space in the context of a deeper Wholeness.

- What sacred stories or sayings come to mind when you think about time and space?
- What values about time and space do you hear articulated in your own spiritual tradition? How do these values shape your experience of time and space?
- In what ways to do these spiritual values support the values of time and space you notice at work? In what ways do they challenge these values?

Respond: The introduction to this conversation suggested that shaping our environments might first mean noticing how our contexts (including our own inner contexts) may be poised for creative change—that is, for transformation.

- Do you notice within yourself or your work context any readiness for transformation with respect to your understanding or use of time or space?
- Are there ways you might facilitate transformation either for yourself or your community?

Bless: As we prepare to return to work or other obligations, offer the person on your left a one- or two-word blessing.

III: How does language shape our values?

Center: Reflect for a moment on your last few days at work, picturing any high or low moments. As you breathe in and out, release these moments or situations to divine Mystery. Breathe out any tension you feel with the word *release*. Breathe in deep peace with the word *peace*. Repeat silently as your breathe: *release . . . peace . . . release . . . peace.*

Check in: Can you share something about the action step you chose as a result of a recent conversation? If you prefer, share whatever you are currently most and least grateful for at work.

Focus: The ways language is used at work can communicate important things about our workplace culture and values. We might begin simply by reflecting on the way language has formed our own attitudes and assumptions in more personal contexts.
- Can you recall a favorite proverb or saying—positive or negative— of someone important to you as a young person, perhaps a teacher, relative, coach, or mentor?
- What are the favorite expressions in your family system now?
- What did/do these sayings communicate about what's most important within the given context?

Reflect: In the workplace, too, of course, language communicates what's important. Words certainly do this, but so do nonverbal forms of "language" such as images or expressions.
- What are the favorite buzzwords or expressions in your workplace at the moment?
- What are the key words or phrases used to describe your organization's work or mission?

- What images shape your organization's self-understanding?
- Can you recall an interaction with a colleague in which the nonverbal aspect of the communication was central to the message?
- How does language communicate and shape the culture and values of your workplace?
- Do you ever feel a disconnect at work between the values expressed and those practiced?

Connect: Let's turn now to our spiritual values as expressed through words, images, and ritual—in the language of our faith traditions.
- Which words or phrases from your tradition most inform or shape your self-understanding?
- What images or rituals most powerfully express the values of your tradition?
- How do you live out your spiritual values at work? How does your language express these values?
- Do you ever feel a disconnect between your spiritual values and the values of your workplace? Between how you'd *like* to act at work and how you *have* to act at work? Between the language you use and language you'd like to use? How would using language differently change your work context?

Respond: Language may shape our own self-understanding and the cultures of which we're a part, but it's also true that we are co-creators of those cultures and of that understanding.
- How might you live your spiritual values more fully within the workplace?
- Where you discover a disconnect between espoused values and lived values, are there things you can do to become more congruent?
- How might you be more mindful of the ways language shapes self-understanding and behavior?

Bless: As we prepare to return to work or other obligations, offer the person on your left a one- or two-word blessing.

IV: Can values be managed?

Center: Reflect for a moment on your last few days at work, picturing any high or low moments. As you breathe in and out, release these moments or situations to divine Mystery. Breathe out any tension you feel with the word *release*. Breathe in deep peace with the word *peace*. Repeat silently as your breathe: *release . . . peace . . . release . . . peace.*

Check in: Can you share something about an action step you've been working on recently? Or would you share whatever work-related concern is most on your mind at the moment?

Focus: Charles McCoy, for many years a senior fellow at the Center for Ethics and Social Policy in Berkeley, California, worked with some of the world's largest corporations in the area of ethics and policy making. In his book, *Management of Values*, McCoy suggests that corporate or professional decisions are always informed ethically; that is, values of some sort determine policy. The process is not always intentional, however. Read the excerpt on page 36 from McCoy's consulting experience.

Now recall a time in your own professional experience when an important decision was made to which you were either a party or of which you were a close observer:
- What values came into play in the decision-making process?
- Was the process of "ethical reflection" conscious or unconscious, overt or covert?
- Generally speaking, how do decisions get made in your workplace?

Reflect: McCoy discusses the importance of the "environment of values" within which decisions are made. By this he means "both the environment that is internal to the company and the environment that surrounds it,"[1] including the specific profession or industry in general, the government and social agencies related to it, and, of course, the wider society.
- What can you say about the "internal environment of values" where you work?
- Are there core values that inform your workplace decisions?
- How do these core values play into the decisions you make at work?
- What about the "external environment of values" in which you work?

Connect/Respond: We may not feel we have much power to transform the "environment of values" of our whole profession or organization, but we may have more influence than we realize in shaping the values of the smaller work team or workplace community in which we spend most of our time.
- What insights have emerged from today's conversation, and how might you apply these at your workplace?
- How might you become more intentional about how your values play into your decision making at work?

■ Do you ever notice a disconnect between your stated values and your values as you live them at work, between what you believe and what you do?
■ What spiritual practices might help you stay aware of your own core values?
■ What small step could you take to shape the values of your workplace?

Bless: As we prepare to leave today's conversation, offer the person on your left a one- or two-word blessing.

Values and Business: An Anecdote[2]

"Ethics is not something we deal with in business operation," Tom told me. "All the people I work with are, I'm sure, thoroughly ethical in their business practices, and we certainly are not going to check on people's private morals unless there was some clear impact on their professional capabilities. But we can't afford ethics in our loan policies. That would be giving the store away. We have to go for the bottom line. There's no other way."

Tom is a senior executive in a bank well up in the top 20. We were sitting in his office, high in the firm's skyscraper headquarters. He was the first of several top managers that the corporation's CEO had asked me to talk with as preparation for a corporate ethics seminar.

"Let's see what Bill says about ethics and business. It's time for our interview with him now," Tom continued. . . . "Bill manages our entire real estate loan division. He is the hardest-nosed person here when it comes to profits."

Bill's secretary . . . escorted us into an office with a spectacular vista of harbor and bridges. . . .

"Would you make any kind of loan that would produce a big profit?" I asked Bill when we had been introduced and the three of us were settled comfortably . . . [in] his office.

"That's what we're here for, to make money," Bill responded, "and I always take that into account. But that doesn't mean we would make *any* kind of loan to turn a buck. For one thing, we have our reputation to consider. We've been around a while, so people respect and trust us. Without that, we'd be dead in the water."

"So you do have other criteria for making loans besides maximizing profits?" I queried.

"Sure, that's always necessary," he agreed, "but then, it would be [a] matter of long-range versus immediate profit."

"I hear there's lots to be made financing casinos in Vegas, Reno, and Atlantic City," Tom said. "We must have quite a bundle invested in those places."

Bill's eyes narrowed slightly as he turned toward Tom. "We don't have a dime in casinos anywhere, and we won't as long as I'm running this division."

"Why is that?" Tom asked, somewhat puzzled.

"Two reasons, basically," Bill replied without hesitation. "First, I don't think it fits in with what this company stands for. And second, those places poison the social atmosphere all of us live in. No way."

Back in his office, Tom confessed to me that Bill's response . . . took him by surprise. . . . "Maybe," I suggested, "you and Bill and others here are making all sorts of value judgments without discussing them among yourselves . . . or being aware . . . of the criteria shaping your policy-making process."

"That's possible," Tom answered thoughtfully, ". . . we may have more ethics here than I thought."

"Yes," I said. . . . "If ethical reflection is the process of selecting the values used in making policy, you and your colleagues who manage this corporation are clearly deeply engaged in ethics. You can discuss this process or you can let it operate covertly as with Bill and casino loans. The real choice is whether to fly blind or to be clear about the ways you set priorities and determine the values that control corporate policy. I would think you'd want to manage values as carefully as you manage financial affairs."

"I'm beginning to see why our president wants us to discuss ethics . . . ," he said as . . . I was leaving.

Notes

1. Charles S. McCoy, *Management of Values: The Ethical Difference in Corporate Policy and Performance* (New York: Harper & Row, 1985), 48.
2. Ibid., 29–31.

meaning-making at work

I: Can we consecrate the ordinary?

Center: Let yourself relax, closing your eyes if you wish. Breathe deeply, and notice any tension in your body. Stay with it a moment, and then relax it. Notice your feelings and thoughts, letting them be within your soul. Become aware that divine Mystery surrounds you, inviting you to a deeper wholeness, "containing" your thoughts and feelings, the events of the morning, the present moment—everything—within that wholeness.

Check in: Can you share something about the action step you chose as a result of a recent conversation? If you prefer, share whatever you are currently most and least grateful for at work.

Focus: We are beginning a series of conversations about meaning-making, looking at the ways our understanding shapes and even transforms our experience. Since work fills much of our time, its meaning is of no small importance. And yet most of us reflect only rarely on its meaning and much, maybe most, of what we do may seem rather mundane. In *Kitchen Table Wisdom,* Rachel Remen muses about "Consecrating the Ordinary" (see the excerpt on page 41). Listen as her reflection is read. What images, thoughts, memories, feelings are evoked in you as you listen? Note any phrases that especially strike you as significant.

■ Does Remen's reflection connect in any way with your own experience of life and work?

■ What images or memories were recalled to your mind by the reading?

Reflect/Connect: In the final paragraph of her essay, Dr. Remen suggests that if we open up to it, all of life can become a ritual in which we meet the sacred, in which we see What Is already there, "deeply hidden in the obvious." Re-read this paragraph for yourself, recalling and reflecting for a moment your own work life and the workplace rituals that punctuate your days.

■ Can you muse aloud about your experience of your own workdays as "ritual?"

■ Are there places where the sacred may lie "deeply hidden in the obvious?" What keeps us from noticing?

■ When you think of the Divine in your workplace, what images come to your mind?

Respond: "Consecrating the ordinary" doesn't just happen; it requires an act of will. How might you begin such "consecration" this week? Here are some possibilities:

1. Select some routine moment or task of your workday. Reflect on how you might consecrate this "ritual."
2. Pick some ordinary space in your workplace—the coffee room or an elevator, for example—and "consecrate" it, determining that you will regard it as "holy ground." When you enter it, expect to meet the Divine there and pay attention to what happens.
3. Recall or find a prayer or psalm from the wisdom of your spiritual tradition and bring it to work. Pray it in your own office space daily. Notice whether and how its meaning changes and whether or how it changes the meaning of your work.
4. Pause mid-day to reflect on your morning asking, "How have my daily habits awakened me this morning?" You might write out this question or something similar, placing it where you're sure to see it. Do the same as you are leaving work.

Is there one of these you might be willing to try this week? Or how else might you apply the insights of today's conversation to your own work situation?

Bless: Share a one- or two-word blessing with the person on your left.

From "Consecrating the Ordinary" in *Kitchen Table Wisdom*, by Rachel Naomi Remen[1]

As you listen to this reading, notice what images, thoughts, memories, feelings are evoked in you.

It is said that the Christian mystic Theresa of Avila found difficulty at first in reconciling the vastness of the life of the spirit with the mundane tasks of her Carmelite convent: the washing of pots, the sweeping of floors, the folding of laundry. At some point of grace, the mundane became for her a sort of prayer, a way she could experience her ever-present connection to the divine pattern that is the source of life. She began then to see the face of God in the folded sheets.

People can most easily recognize mystery when it presents itself in dramatic ways: the person who heals for unknown reasons when all hope is gone, the angelic visitation, the life-altering coincidence. We seem to be able to hear God best when He shouts—even Moses required a burning bush, and Jesus' disciples needed him to feed multitudes with a single fish. Yet mystery is as common as a trip to the grocery store. In *Guide for the Perplexed*, E. F. Schumacher notes that the endless debate about the nature of the world is founded on difference in the sensitivity of the eyes that behold it: "We can see only what we have grown an eye to see." Some of us can only notice miracles. Some of us can only see in times of crisis. Yet we can all learn to see God in the folded sheets.

Soon after I moved to California from New York, I planted a vegetable garden. I had never seen fresh vegetables except in a supermarket, and the first year I found an endless fascination in this tiny garden. I especially loved the lettuce, which I had planted tightly in a square whose edges I harvested for dinner every night. One evening I had gone out to pick the salad as usual and ran a hand lightly over the crisp green square of lettuce leaves, marveling at its vitality, almost as if it were bubbling up out of the ground. Suddenly words from my childhood came back to me, words that I had heard countless times over the dinner tables of aunts and uncles and knew by heart, words that I heard now for the first time:

Blessed art Thou, O Lord, King of the universe who bringest forth bread from the earth.

Far from being the usual meaningless mumble, these words suddenly were a potent description of something real, a statement about grace and the mystery of life itself. Up until then I had taken this blessing as a theory or a hypothesis, someone's idea of how things worked. I had no idea that these familiar words were simply a description of something true. I had never witnessed them happening in the world before.

I had done ritual the way I had done life. Automatically. Life can become habit, something done without thinking. Living life in this way does not awaken us. Yet any of our daily habits can awaken us. All of life can become ritual. When it does, our experience of life changes radically and the ordinary becomes consecrated. Ritual doesn't make mystery happen. It helps us see and experience something which is already real. It does not create the sacred, it only describes what is there and has always been there, deeply hidden in the obvious.

Note

1. Rachel Naomi Remen, *Kitchen Table Wisdom: Stories That Heal* (New York: Riverhead Books, 1996), 282–84.

II: *Money and meaning*

Center: Let yourself relax, closing your eyes if you wish. Breathe deeply, and notice any tension in your body. Stay with it a moment, and then relax it. Notice your feelings and thoughts, letting them be within your soul. Become aware that divine Mystery surrounds you, inviting you to a deeper wholeness, "containing" your thoughts and feelings, the events of the morning, the present moment—everything—within that wholeness.

Check in: Can you share something about a recent action step or a work-related concern?

Focus: As we continue our conversations about meaning-making, we look today at one of the most powerful meaning-makers in our culture: money. Consider for a moment your own history with money and its meaning, reflecting on the turning points and changes that have occurred through the years. Think about:
1. Your earliest experiences with money as a child.
2. The meaning money had for you as a teenager or young adult.
3. The experience of your first paycheck.
4. Other memorable moments relating to money.
5. Your attitude toward money now.

■ Can you share a memory or anecdote that captures your earliest experience with money?
■ What meaning did money have for you as you grew older?
■ What two or three words might you use to summarize the meaning money has for you at the present time?

Reflect: In *Secular Sanctity,* Father Edward Hays, a Roman Catholic priest, writes of the sacramental nature of money. If a sacrament is an external sign of an inner reality, then the way we use our money is a manifestation of who we are. An excerpt from his book begins below. Let's read it silently, reflecting on our own current understanding and experience of money. If you wish, jot down specific ways your own experience illustrates or contradicts what Hays writes.

- What connections do you make between what Hays writes and your own experience?
- At what points do you agree/disagree with Hays?
- How is money a "sacrament" of who you are and/or what you believe?
- Does the way you use money accurately reflect who you are and what you most value?

Connect/Respond: While most of us reflect periodically on how we will spend our money, much of the time we spend automatically, without much thought. Becoming more mindful of money as a sacrament may help us connect who we are, what we do, and what we believe. This week you might:

1. For one day, become more mindful of how you spend money and how you feel as you spend it. If possible, keep a log, and at the end of the day, reflect on how your expenditures were "sacramental."
2. Review your personal budget in light of Hays' reflections.
3. Look at the budget of your department or organization. How does this budget reflect its values?
4. Identify appropriate wisdom and meditate on the meaning money has within your spiritual tradition.

Is there one of these you might be willing to try this week? Or how else might you apply the insights of today's conversation to your own experience with money?

Bless: Share a one- or two-word blessing with the person on your left.

From *Secular Sanctity,* by Edward Hays[1]

First, we should love our money and take pride in it. It is good to be proud of having earned it, for money is one sign of a job well done. Every paycheck is a pat on the back.

Next, mindful that our money is a sacrament in which we can say, "This is me . . . this is my sweat and toil . . . ," we should use it to nourish our bodies, which it represents. So, part of our income goes for food, clothing, shelter and also for entertainment and fun. This expression of self-love is good and holy.

The dollar bills in your billfold are not only a sign of you, but also of the community to which you belong. They are the frequent reminder that you belong to a certain nation whose money you use symbolically. So, with part of your money you pay taxes. You should rejoice that this communion of self helps to build highways, pay teachers' salaries and patch up the potholes in the street in front of your house. . . .

Some of your money goes into our Social Security system and is given to the elderly and the needy. So, a part of you puts food on the plate of some aged man or woman or helps pay the rent of an elderly person. By means of this withholding payment you are able to put flesh on the words that Jesus speaks about seeing him in those who are in need. . . .

Finally, in numerous ways we are inclined to use parts of our money on gifts to those we love, to friends and to those organizations and activities we feel are important to the world and to growth of the human spirit. Whenever we give a gift of money we could seal it with a kiss or a wink . . . saying, "This is my body . . . this is me . . . this is my love."

Note

1. Edward Hays, *Secular Sanctity* (Leavenworth, Kansas: Forest of Peace Publishing House, 1984), 41.

III: Job or work?

Center: Let yourself relax, closing your eyes if you wish. Breathe deeply, and notice any tension in your body. Stay with it a moment, and then relax it. Notice your feelings and thoughts, letting them be within your soul. Become aware that divine Mystery surrounds you, inviting you to a deeper wholeness, "containing" your thoughts and feelings, the events of the day, the present moment—everything—within that wholeness.

Check in: Can you share something about a recent action step you've taken? Or, what has been most life-giving or life-draining in your workweek so far?

Focus/Reflect: Matthew Fox, in his book *The Reinvention of Work,* makes a useful distinction between *job* and *work:*[1]

Job: . . . the now obsolete word *jobbe* meant 'piece.' . . . Job denotes a discrete task, and one that is not very joyful. The Middle English word *gobbe,* from which job is derived, meant 'lump.' In his eighteenth century dictionary, Dr. Johnson defined *job* as: 'petty, piddling work; a piece of chance work.'

Work: comes from inside out; work is the expression of our soul, our inner being. It is unique to the individual; it is creative. Work is an expression of the Spirit at work in the world through us. Work is that which puts us in touch with others . . . at the level of service in the community.

- Can you give examples from your own life of both job and work as described by Fox?
- What words or images capture for you job and work?
- What's important about a job? About work?
- Why do we take jobs? Why do we work?

Connect: Matthew Fox goes on to write, "Given a deep spirituality, one can turn even a job into work, re-envisioning its place in the whole." Fox seems to imply here that turning a job into work may have something to do with placing what we do in a wider context. In any case, such a shift may involve some sort of reframing of the job's meaning. The spiritual wisdom of many traditions invites this reframing. Let's take a few minutes to read and reflect on the quotations and questions on page 46.

- What clues do you find in these quotations that might help you discover ways to transform job into work in your own life?
- Have you discovered your own strategies for understanding the jobs you do as work?

Respond: Beginning to turn a job into work may require an act of will. This week you might:
1. Select one of the quotes on the back and reflect daily on the question it suggests.
2. Find a colleague at work with whom to discuss today's conversation.
3. Identify one job you are currently stuck with, and reflect on and experiment with ways it might become work for you.
4. Make a chart in which you list jobs on one side and work on the other; generate a third list of ways you might incorporate the work into each job.

Is there one of these you might be willing to try this week? Or how else might you apply the insights of today's conversation to your own experience with money?

Bless: Share a one- or two-word blessing with the person on your left.

Thoughts on Job vs. Work:
Quotes and Questions

Take a moment to reflect on each of these, jotting down any thoughts or images that occur to you.

> Offer to me all thy works and rest thy mind on the Supreme. Be free from vain hopes and selfish thoughts, and with inner peace fight thou thy fight.[2]
> —the Bahagavad Gita

What would it look like for you to "fight thou thy fight . . . with inner peace?"

> Do your work, then step back.
> The only path to serenity . . .
> He who clings to his work
> will create nothing that endures.
> If you want to accord with the Tao,
> just do your job, then let go.[3]
> —Tao Te Ching

How might you "do your work and then step back?"

> . . . do not worry saying, 'What will we eat? or 'What will we drink?' . . . your heavenly Father knows that you need all these things. But strive first for the kingdom of God and his righteousness, and all these things will be given to you as well.[4]
> —Christian Scriptures

What would striving for . . . "his righteousness" look like in your workplace?

> The outward work can never be small if the inward one is great, and the outward work can never be great or good if the inward is small or of little worth. The inward work always includes in itself all size, all breadth and all length.[5]
> —Meister Eckhart

What sort of "inner work" might be related to the "outer work" of your workplace?

> My occupation: Love. That's all I do.[6]
> —St. John of the Cross

What would "love" look like in your work?

Notes

1. Matthew Fox, *The Reinvention of Work: A New Vision of Livelihood for Our Time* (San Francisco: Harper, 1994), 5–6.

2. *The Bahagavad Gita,* trans. Juan Mascaro (Middlesex, England: Penguin, 1962), 58, 59.

3. Tao Te Ching, trans. Stephen Mitchell (New York: Harper & Row, 1988), 9, 24.

4. Matthew 6:31–33, NRSV.

5. Matthew Fox, *Breakthrough: Meister Eckhart's Creation Spirituality in New Translation* (New York: Doubleday, 1980), 257.

6. St. John of the Cross, *The Poems of St. John of the Cross,* trans. John Frederick Nims (Chicago: University of Chicago Press, 1979), 9.

IV: Can our work be sacred?

Center: Let yourself relax, closing your eyes if you wish. Breathe deeply, and notice any tension in your body. Stay with it a moment, and then relax it. Notice your feelings and thoughts, letting them be within your soul. Become aware that divine Mystery surrounds you, inviting you to a deeper wholeness, "containing" your thoughts and feelings, the events of the day, the present moment—everything—within that wholeness.

Check in: Can you share something about an action step you've been working on recently? Or would you share whatever work-related concern is most on your mind at the moment?

Focus/Reflect: Today we conclude our series on meaning-making at work. Even when we don't have much control over the work itself, we *can* determine the meaning we make of our work—the way we understand its import. Frederic and Mary Ann Brussat, in their book *Spiritual Literacy: Reading the Sacred in Everyday Life,* suggest that "With creativity and imagination, it is possible to reframe any . . . work and see it as a partnership with God in the ongoing creation of the world."[1] They offer as an example a story told by Rabbi Jeffrey Salkin on page 48. Let's begin by reflecting on the meaning of our own work in light of this story.

- How does Rabbi Salkin's story connect with your own experience of work?
- How might you understand your own work as "a sacred mission?"
- Can you recall a situation in your own workplace in which you or someone else was a "connector?"

Connect: Sometimes it is easier to see the work of another as a "sacred mission" than to understand our own this way. One way to learn the art of re-framing might be to reflect on our work each day using three simple questions suggested by Angeles Arrien:

1. What surprised me today?
2. What moved me today?
3. What inspired me today?

In answering these questions, we may be able to spot the presence of the Divine in our work and get a sense of our work as "sacred mission." Let's take a moment to reflect on our own work experiences so far this week, answering these three questions. If you wish, jot down a note or two.

■ Can you share one or more of the answers to Arrien's three questions?
■ As you reflect on these experiences now, do you have any sense of how the Divine might have been present in them?

Respond: Understanding our work as "sacred mission" requires a certain purposefulness on our part, a willingness to open ourselves. We might begin by trying one of the following:

1. Keep a journal in which you record each day, in a sentence or two, the answers to the three simple questions as a way to train yourself to spot the presence of the Divine.
2. As you begin each workday, use some simple ritual of your own, choosing to remind yourself that your work is a "sacred mission."
3. Pause at lunch to "map" the possible ways you acted as a "connector" during the morning.
4. Seek out a colleague or two at work and invite them to share the meaning they make of their own work.

Is there one of these you might be willing to try this week? Or how else might you apply the insights of today's conversation to your own work situation?

Bless: Offer the person on your left a word of hope or blessing for the coming week.

From *Being God's Partner*, by Rabbi Jeffrey K. Salkin[2]

A few years ago, a young taxi driver drove me to John F. Kennedy Airport on Long Island. . . .

"So, rabbi," he asked while we sat in heavy traffic, "what do you say to a Jew like me who hasn't been in a synagogue since his bar mitzvah ceremony?"

Thinking a moment, I recalled that in Hasidic lore, the *ball aqalah* (wagon driver) is an honored profession. So I said, "We could talk about your work."

"What does my work have to do with religion?"

"Well, we choose how we look at the world and at life. You're a taxi driver. But you are also a piece of the tissue that connects all humanity. You're taking me to the airport. I'll go to a different city and give a couple of lectures that might touch or help or change someone. I couldn't have gotten there without you. You help make that connection happen.

"I heard on your two-way radio that after you drop me off, you're going to pick up a woman from the hospital and take her home. That means that you'll be the first non-medical person she encounters after being in a hospital. You will be a small part of her healing process, an agent in her re-entry into the world of health.

"You may then pick up someone from the train station who has come home from seeing a dying parent. You may take someone to the house of the one that he or she will ask to join in marriage. You're a connector, a bridge builder. You're one of the unseen people who make the world work as well as it does. That is holy work. You may not think of it this way, but yours is a sacred mission."

Notes

1. Frederic and Mary Ann Brussat, *Spiritual Literacy: Reading the Sacred in Everyday Life* (New York: Scribner, 1996), 308.

2. Jeffery K. Salkin, *Being God's Partner: How to Find the Hidden Links Between Spirituality and Your Work* (Woodstock, Vermont: Jewish Lights Publishing, 1994), 170–71.

time and its meaning

I: "Time's a wastin'"—What makes time truly productive?

Center: Pause for a moment, closing your eyes if you wish, relaxing your body and taking a few deep breaths. Listen to a phrase from the Hebrew scripture: "This is the day the Lord has made." Reflect for a moment on your own day so far in light of this phrase. Again: "This is the day the Lord has made." Finally: "This is the day the Lord has made; let us rejoice and be glad in it."

Check in: Can you share something about an action step you've been working on recently? Or would you share whatever work-related concern is most on your mind at the moment?

Focus: Our culture is almost obsessed with time: finding enough of it, making the most of it, saving more of it. But even with all the attention we give it, we're rarely truly mindful of how we spend it; we rarely reflect on the values our choices about time reflect. Today we begin a four-session consideration of time, beginning our conversation with a look at "productive" time. Let's begin with our own experience. Read over the following questions and start with the one that seems most compelling:

- Can you recall an experience of using your time in a truly productive way? What was this like for you?
- Have you ever had the experience of fearing something would be "a waste of time" and then found it to be time well spent after all?
- When was the last time you went ahead and did something you wanted to do even though you really didn't have time for it? What was the outcome?
- In your life, what or who has influenced your understanding of productive versus wasted time?

Reflect: The way we spend our time—like the way we spend our money—reflects what we most deeply value. Looking at the situations about which we've just shared:

- What was produced in each situation?
- What was wasted?
- What values are reflected in each situation?

Connect: One of the best-known reflections about time comes from the Hebrew wisdom literature. Take a moment to read it on page 53.

- What values or insights about time are reflected in this passage?
- Which one of the times listed in this passage most closely describes your own current time?
- How does this passage speak to the observations about time we've made today?
- If you were to make your own work-related list of "for everything there is a time," what would you include?

Respond: One of the greatest challenges relating to time may be simply to become more mindful of how we use it. We might focus our action steps on time-related mindfulness. You might, for example:

1. Take a few minutes at the end of the day to reflect on your use of time and the values expressed in your time-related decisions for that day.
2. Make a list of five "a time to _____ and a time to _____" phrases, and reflect on the amount of time you spent on each for a given day or week.
3. Find at least one occasion to "waste time" during your work week; see what, if anything, productive results.

Is there one of these you might be willing to try this week? Or how else might you apply the insights of today's conversation to your own work situation?

Bless: Offer the person on your left a word of hope or blessing for the coming week.

Ecclesiastes 3:1–11a from the Hebrew Bible

For everything there is a season, and a time for every matter under
  heaven:
a time to be born, and a time to die;
a time to plant, and a time to pluck up what is planted;
a time to kill, and a time to heal;
a time to break down, and a time to build up;
a time to weep, and a time to laugh;
a time to mourn, and a time to dance;
a time to throw away stones, and a time to gather stones together;
a time to embrace, and a time to refrain from embracing;
a time to seek, and a time to lose;
a time to keep, and a time to throw away;
a time to tear, and a time to sew;
a time to keep silence, and a time to speak;
a time to love, and a time to hate;
a time for war and a time for peace.

What gain have the workers from their toil? I have seen the business
that God has given to everyone to be busy with. He has made everything
suitable for its time.

II: "For the time being"—What can we do about how busy we are?

Center: Pause for a moment, closing your eyes if you wish, relaxing your
body and taking a few deep breaths. Listen to a phrase from the Hebrew
scripture: "This is the day the Lord has made." Reflect for a moment on
your own day so far in light of this phrase. Again: "This is the day the Lord
has made." Finally: "This is the day the Lord has made; let us rejoice and
be glad in it."

Check in: Can you share something about a recent action step or a work-
related concern?

Focus: Our culture, for all its time-saving innovations, still seems to be "time starved." We never seem to have enough time to do all we want or need to do. Today we continue our consideration of time by looking at our busy-ness. As we often do, let's begin with our own experience:

- Can you recall a time recently when you felt overwhelmed with all you had to do? What was this like for you?
- When was the last time you felt truly relaxed, free of time pressures? What was this like?
- Can you recall a time when you said "yes" to a request for your time when you really needed to say "no?"

Reflect: Last time we talked a little about the values that underlie our decisions about time. Of course, choosing to act on some values means choosing not to act on others. Other factors having a powerful, sometimes unconscious, impact on our decisions about time are our values and emotions. Consider each of these as you reflect on the situations and decisions you've just shared.

- What values prompted your decisions to spend your time as you did?
- In saying "yes" to the expression of some values, to what values were you then saying "no?"
- What emotions came into play in the time decisions you've talked about today?
- What emotions are connected to the values you hold about your use of time?

Connect: A prayer from the Hebrew Bible contains these words, "My times are in your hand . . ." (Psalm 31:15). Let's pause for a moment and reflect silently (for a minute or two) on our conversation in light of these brief words of wisdom. As you meditate, visualize some of the recent time decisions you've made, repeating this phrase to yourself as you visualize or reflect on them.

- What thought or meaning occurs to you about time in light of this wisdom?
- What wisdom regarding time from your own spiritual tradition might be helpful to us here?

Respond: Perhaps one of the greatest challenges relating to time is simply to become more mindful of how we use it. We might focus our action steps on time-related "mindfulness." You might, for example:

1. Sometime during the week, take a few minutes at the end of the day to reflect on your use of time and the values expressed in your time-related decisions for that day.

2. Several times during the week, meditate on "My times are in your hand."

3. Be especially mindful when someone asks you to do something this week: what are you feeling; what values are reflected in your response to the request for your time?

4. List the time commitments you've made, the values each reflects, and the emotions involved in your decisions to make each commitment. Over several days, gently meditate on your list to see what emerges for you.

Is there one of these you might be willing to try this week? Or how else might you apply the insights of today's conversation to your own life or work?

Bless: Offer the person on your left a word of hope or blessing for the coming week.

III: "Time and time again"—Is ours the only way to look at time?

Center: Pause for a moment, closing your eyes if you wish, relaxing your body and taking a few deep breaths. Listen to a phrase from the Hebrew scripture: "This is the day the Lord has made." Reflect for a moment on your own day so far in light of this phrase. Again: "This is the day the Lord has made." Finally: "This is the day the Lord has made; let us rejoice and be glad in it."

Check in: Can you share something of a recent action step? If you prefer, share what has been most life-giving or life-draining about your workweek so far.

Focus: Our culture tends to view time as a resource or commodity: we spend it, save it, invest it, waste it, and so on. Almost any term we apply to the use of financial resources, we also apply to time. Other societies, however, may understand time differently. They may be more relaxed about it, understand or value it differently. Reflect for a moment on the variety of "times" you have experienced in your life, at home, at work, and elsewhere.

■ Have you had the opportunity to experience time in another culture? What was this like?

- Can you recall the way time flowed when you were a child? What story or memory from childhood or youth captures your experience of time?
- What images come to mind when you think of the way you currently experience time? At work? At home?
- How has your experience of time changed throughout your life journey?

Reflect: Time in our own culture tends to be linear, "rational." As a way of seeing time from a new perspective, it might be useful to experiment with non-linear strategies for entering our experience of time. Choose one of the following "mini-exercises" and take a few moments to work with it privately, using a notebook or some space on this agenda:

1. Jot down some word images or a brief "poem" about how you experience time.
2. Create a "doodle" that captures in an image your current feelings about time.
3. Close your eyes and meditate on the meaning of time in your life; pay special attention to how your body reacts: where do you tense as you reflect on time, what happens with your breathing?

- What was your emotional response to the exercise?
- What did you learn about your own experience of time?

Connect/Respond: A discernment tool we often use as part of our check-in asks the question: "What in our lives is life-giving or life-draining?" In this way, we may come closer to discerning the presence of Spirit in our activities, in our "times," and closer to discerning how the Divine is inviting us to lives of greater wholeness. With respect to the stories, images, and thoughts we've shared today:

- Have any of these ways of experiencing time been especially life-giving or life-draining?
- Can you recall an especially life-giving experience of time? In what way was Spirit present in the experience? What divine invitation was hidden in the experience?
- What might you do this week to become more mindful of your life-giving and/or life-draining relationships to time?

Bless: Offer the person on your left a word of hope or blessing for the coming week.

IV: *"In the fullness of time"—When is Spirit at work in our time?*

Center: Pause for a moment, closing your eyes if you wish, relaxing your body and taking a few deep breaths. Listen to a phrase from the Hebrew scripture: "This is the day the Lord has made." Reflect for a moment on your own day so far in light of this phrase. Again: "This is the day the Lord has made." Finally: "This is the day the Lord has made; let us rejoice and be glad in it."

Check in: Can you share something about the action step you chose as a result of a recent conversation? If you prefer, share whatever you are currently most and least grateful for at work.

Focus: This week we conclude our conversations about time. For the most part, we regard time as a "measurable duration": a sequence of moments or events. But there *are* times when such an ordinary conception of time doesn't quite capture our experience. Let's consider such moments:

- Can you recall a time when you were poised on the edge of an important decision; when you sensed "it's now or never?" What was this like for you?
- Have you ever had the experience of being so fully engaged in what you were doing that you forgot time?
- Can you share a story about a time when you were involved in a project or event in which everything just seemed to come together, in which paradoxically you were both working hard and watching things flow effortlessly into place?

Reflect: The ancient Greeks had a number of words for time. Ordinary "clock time" was *chronos,* but a second word for time, *kairos,* connoted several deeper meanings, such as those decisive moments when something special was possible, immanent: "pregnant time." *Kairos* was also used to describe "time out of time," transcendent time in which time is filled and, in a sense, fulfilled.

- How do the stories we've just been telling reflect *chronos* and/or *kairos?*
- How is the experience of each sort of time life-giving or life-draining for you?
- What factors contribute to our experiencing time as *chronos* or *kairos?*
- In your own experience or in others you've had, does *kairos* "just happen," or are there ways in which it can be chosen?

Connect: The Hebrew and Christian scriptures imply that the Divine is present in moments experienced as *kairos,* even that the Divine is the source of such moments.

- In what ways have you felt the presence of Spirit in your own "kairotic" experience, either at decisive moments or in the midst of fulfilled time?
- Can you recall any stories or sayings from your spiritual tradition that might be relevant to our conversation?

Respond: The experience of *kairos* can be immensely satisfying. In our action steps this week we might reflect on ways to make more of our time "kairotic." You might consider trying one of these:

1. Keep a time journal for two or three days in which you reflect on how you've experienced time in various life contexts.
2. Make a time-line of decisive moments in your life, noting any pattern or direction that emerges.
3. Choose a passage from a spiritual text relating to time—perhaps a phrase from the agendas in this series—and use it as the basis for your meditation this week.

Is there one of these actions you'd be willing to experiment with this week? How else might you apply the insights of today's conversation to your work life?

Bless: Offer the person on your left a word of hope or blessing for the coming week.

connecting money with meaning

I: *Money and our identity*

Center: Breathe deeply and let any tension in your body drain through your feet and into the floor. Breathe deeply once again and become aware of divine Presence within and around you. In whatever way is most helpful to you, open yourself to this Presence.

Check in: Can you share something about a recent action step or a work-related concern?

Focus: Money plays a powerful role in our lives, in obvious and not-so-obvious ways. Today we begin a series of conversations in which we look at the spiritual nature of money, that is, the relationship of money to our values, our identity, and other non-material aspects of our lives. In his book, *Money and the Meaning of Life,* Jacob Needleman explores, among other things, the relationship between identity and money. Let's start our own conversation by reflecting together about our associations with money:

- Can you recall a situation from your distant or recent past in which money was connected with a strong positive emotion (joy, satisfaction, love, etc.)? A strong negative emotion (anxiety, anger, guilt, etc.)?

■ How is your sense of self or self-respect influenced by or related to money?

■ What questions about money, values, and self-identity have surfaced for you through the years?

Reflect: Human beings are both spiritual and material creatures, our identity both spiritual and physical. We long for connection with what is Greater than ourselves, *and* we live and work in a physical, material world, struggling with practical, everyday needs and wants. Needleman suggests that conscious, objective reflection on the place of money in our lives can unify these two sides of our identity since such reflection can make very clear the connection—or lack of connection—between what we believe and how we actually act in the everyday world. After you read the first excerpt on page 61, let's begin to explore these connections:

■ What do you notice about the separation of your spiritual and material lives?

■ In what ways does your use of money reflect your deepest values?

■ How does your use of money sometimes fail to reflect these values?

■ What prevents you from using your money in ways that would more clearly reflect what's most important to you?

Connect: The Christian scriptures seem to suggest that one's relationship to money can be spiritually tricky, pointing to the compelling way money can hold and even oppress us. On the other hand, it's not money itself, but the *love* of money that seems to corrupt. Look over the quotations from these scriptures on page 62 and then consider these questions:

■ What do you know of the dilemma of "serving two masters"? Or of money as the "root of all kinds of evil"?

■ What antidote to the love of money is implied in these passages?

■ In your own experience, how is money related to one's identity?

■ What does your own spiritual tradition suggest as an appropriate foundation for one's identity?

Respond: As we often do, let's consider how we might begin to apply the insights of today's conversation to our lives. You might, for example:

1. Buy a copy of Needleman's book and reflect personally on the questions it raises.

2. Reflect on the questions we've discussed today by journaling about them.

3. Engage colleagues, friends, or family in a conversation about today's topic.
4. Write a money autobiography tracing your feelings, attitudes, and life events related to money.
5. Keep track of expenditures for a day or two, making a list at the end of each day, recording the personal value reflected in each expenditure (e.g. "food—family;" "shelter—family," "self-care," "work-related," "service/charity to others," etc.).

Is there one of these you might be willing to try this week? How else might you apply the insights of today's conversation to your own life?

Bless: As we prepare to return to work, offer the person on your left a brief word of hope or blessing.

From "Lightning Flashes," the introduction to the paperback edition of *Money and the Meaning of Life,* by Jacob Needleman[1]

The effort to study the money question ... with a "warm objectivity," brings one toward a fresh observation of nearly the whole of one's life.... Without consciousness of the part of ourselves that is involved with money, we run the risk of becoming moral or spiritual beings with only half of our nature—and therefore not really moral or spiritual at all. The money question becomes, therefore, a nearly indispensable help in bringing ... unity [into our lives. ...] The part of ourselves that must ... live our life in the material world needs to be embraced with the same attention that seeks contact with higher forces and ideals.

- What do you notice about the separation of your spiritual and material lives?
- In what ways does your use of money reflect your deepest spiritual values?
- How does your use of money sometimes fail to reflect these values?
- What gets in the way of your using your money in ways that would more clearly reflect what's most important to you?

From the Christian scriptures:

> No slave can serve two masters; for a slave will either hate the one and love the other, or be devoted to the one and despise the other. You cannot serve God and wealth.
>
> —Luke 16:13, Matthew 6:24

> For the love of money is a root of all kinds of evil, and in their eagerness to be rich some have wandered away from the faith . . .
>
> —I Timothy 6:10

> Keep your lives free from the love of money, and be content with what you have; for [God] has said, 'I will never leave you or forsake you.'
>
> —Hebrews 13:5

Note

1. Jacob Needleman, *Money and the Meaning of Life* (New York: Doubleday, 1994), xi.

II: *The "Energy" of money*

Center: Breathe deeply and let any tension in your body drain through your feet and into the floor. Breathe deeply once again and become aware of divine Presence within and around you. In whatever way is most helpful to you, open yourself to this Presence.

Check in: Can you share something about the action step you chose as a result of a recent conversation? If you prefer, share a high or a low point of your workday or week so far.

Focus: Louis Richmond, in his book *Work as a Spiritual Practice,* uses a curious phrase in reference to money; he speaks of "the energy of money," that is, "money as motivating, inspiring, attractive, seductive, powerful." [1] Today we look at this curious energy and the way it plays out in our own life and work.
- What do you know of money as "motivating, inspiring, attractive, seductive, and powerful"?
- In your own work history, what have you observed about the ways the "energy of money" operates in an organization or workplace culture?

Reflect: The words Richmond used to characterize the "energy of money" are emotional words, suggesting that money carries an emotional charge. In the marketplace it is often the way achievement is acknowledged; the withholding of money can communicate displeasure or even anger. Money can become, then, in some situations the currency of connection or disconnection, a powerful energy indeed. Let's consider this for a moment:

- Can you recall a time, perhaps from you childhood, in which money took on an emotional charge or became a tool for communicating either pride or displeasure?
- In your own work life, what sorts of emotional connections does money create or destroy?
- What other money-emotion associations have you noticed at work?

Connect/Respond: Richmond tells an anecdote that might be useful in helping us make connections between the energy of money and our own deepest selves. An acquaintance of Richmond was the senior and highest paid employee of a small plumbing firm. The firm's owner decided to pay his employees a commission on each new customer they brought in and soon this man topped the others in commission income. After a few months, however, the man went to his boss and suggested the commission money be pooled and shared equally among the employees, explaining that the program had created tensions among the employees. Although it meant the immediate loss of income for the senior employee, in the long run, he felt he actually made more money since the others in the firm seemed to work harder to bring in new clients.

- What were the money-emotion connections in this story? How was the energy of money used by the boss, by his senior employees, by the other employees?
- How does your spirituality inform the "energy of money" as you experience it?
- How might you become more aware of how this energy operates in your own life and work?
- Can you think of ways the energy of money may be used creatively in your workplace?

Bless: As we prepare to return to work, offer the person on your left a brief word of hope or blessing.

Note

1. Lewis Richmond, *Work as a Spiritual Practice: A Practical Buddhist Approach to Inner Growth and Satisfaction on the Job* (NewYork: Broadway Books, 1999), 144.

III: The "Soul" of money

Center: Breathe deeply and let any tension in your body drain through your feet and into the floor. Breathe deeply once again and become aware of divine Presence within and around you. In whatever way is most helpful to you, open yourself to this Presence.

Check in: Share your progress on a recent "action step" or the work-related concern most on your mind at the moment.

Focus: It's no secret that the "profit motive" is central to American corporate culture. Yet, while a healthy return on investment is an entirely appropriate goal, most would say that, in addition to profit, there are other values that are—or should be—vital to the way we do business. Today we look at money and its role both in the marketplace and in our own professional lives.

- Can you give a recent example of the "profit motive" at work in your own organization?
- What are other values that you feel are vital to your organization?
- What does it look like in your own workplace when the drive for profit conflicts with other key values?

Reflect/Connect: In his book *Care of the Soul*, psychologist Thomas Moore considers the role money plays in our work culture, inviting reflection on what he calls "the soul of money." In his chapter "The Economics of the Soul"[1] Thomas Moore makes a number of points about the "soulfulness" of money:

1. Money and work are intimately related but are sometimes split apart in our culture so that "the pleasure of money can take the place of the pleasure of work."
2. "Money is the coinage of our relationship to the community and the world;" it is more than a medium of exchange; it "carries the soul of communal life," including its shadow—that is, those aspects of our life—positive and negative—of which we are least aware.
3. Wealth viewed simply as a defense against poverty (destitution) is not true wealth. The "vow of poverty" taken by many religious communities may promote something closer to the soul of money: "The purpose of the vow is to promote community by owning all things in common." Moore asks, "What if, as a nation, a city, or a neighborhood, to say nothing of the globe, we all took such a vow of poverty?"

4. Both wealth and poverty, then, are meant to connect us to "communal, concrete life."

Let's consider how each of these plays out in our personal or professional experience.

■ Can you share an example of how "the pleasure of money" takes the place of "the pleasure of work"?

■ How does your organization's use of money connect it—creatively or less-than-creatively—with the communities that it touches, such as employees, clients, the wider society?

■ How would you define the "true wealth" of an organization? What does "defense against poverty" look like on an organizational level?

■ What wisdom from your spiritual tradition provides insight into either the soulfulness of money or the shadow of money?

Respond: Money *is* a powerful part of our lives, individually and communally, and becoming more aware of the money's positive and negative "soulfulness" can help us relate to it more creatively.

■ What insights from today's conversation seem especially useful to you?

■ What action step or steps would you be willing to undertake in response to today's conversation?

Bless: As we prepare to return to work, offer the person on your left a brief word of hope or blessing.

Note:

1. Thomas Moore, *Care of the Soul, A Guide for Cultivating Depth and Sacredness in Everyday Living* (New York: HarperPerennial, 1994), 189–96.

IV: The meaning of wealth

Center: Breathe deeply and let any tension in your body drain through your feet and into the floor. Breathe deeply once again and become aware of divine Presence within and around you. In whatever way is most helpful to you, open yourself to this Presence.

Check in: Can you share something about the action step you chose as a result of a recent conversation? If you prefer, share whatever you are currently most and least grateful for at work.

Focus: Today we conclude our reflections on money and meaning, returning to Jacob Needleman's *Money and the Meaning of Life*. In an early chapter, Needleman recounts a formative experience he had as a boy. A child of working-class parents, the young Needleman visited the home of a wealthy little friend who had every toy any child could want or imagine and yet, Needleman recounts, "Instead of looking at [the toys,] he looked at me—with a weak, pathetic smile. Here I was in wonderland and there before me was this . . . sad, little prince. . . . Here was a child who had everything . . . but it was not what he wanted!" This experience came to symbolize for Needleman a paradox of our culture: on the one hand was his father, struggling to obtain the things his friend's family had and embittered by not having them; on the other was the "sad, little prince."[1]

- Does Needleman's story bring to mind any experience from your own life?
- How do *you* experience the paradox of wealth in this society?

Reflect: Needleman goes on to point out that:

> . . . ours is a society that has given material wealth first priority . . . Certainly, human beings have always needed and craved material things. And certainly, human beings have always suffered from greed, but not every culture . . . has measured itself principally by the standard of comfort and safety in the material world . . . we want material wealth more than . . . anything else. . . .[2]

- Do you agree with Needleman that our society has placed material wealth at the top of our priorities?
- What consequences might or do result from such an ordering, in the life of our society? In your own life?

Connect: Needleman himself asks, "What is real wealth?" pointing out that just as individuals make choices about what's important, societies set priorities and make choices, determining for themselves what's fundamental and what's secondary. Needleman goes on to ask, "Is what we call 'wealth' determined only by these fundamental choices, which are usually made under the surface of our awareness? Or . . . do we have the power—perhaps even the duty—to define for ourselves what wealth really means?"[3]

- How would you define "wealth?"
- What wisdom from your own spiritual tradition comes to mind as you consider this question?
- In what ways are you wealthy?

Respond: Let's consider briefly:
- How might we apply the insights of today's conversation to our own lives?
- What specific action steps might we take?

Bless: As we prepare to return to work, offer the person on your left a brief word of hope or blessing.

Notes

1. Jacob Needleman, *Money and the Meaning of Life* (New York: Doubleday, 1994), 20–22.
2. Ibid., 22.
3. Ibid., xiv.

emotions at work

I: Joy—How can we "en-joy" work?

Center: Let yourself relax for a moment, breathing deeply and reflecting on the fact that you are in the presence of divine Mystery. Recall some moment of satisfaction—large or small—you've experienced so far today. Let yourself dwell for a moment in the simple joy of that moment. Let that joy become a sort of light, infusing you and your day. As you recall the rest of your day, let it move with you from one place to another until you arrive at this time and place. When you've arrived here and are ready, open your eyes.

Check in: Can you share something about an action step you've been working on recently? If you prefer, share what about your work you're most and least thankful for at the moment.

Focus: We usually use the verb *enjoy* in a passive sense: we enjoy this or that, noticing what gives us pleasure in the situation. But it could also be helpful to consider "en-joy" in a more active sense, as the purposeful act of bringing joy into a situation. We might begin by reflecting on our own experience of joy, discovering what we can of the "anatomy" of joy.

- Can you recall a recent experience of deep joy?
- What memory of joy can you recall from your youth or childhood?
- When have you experienced joy in everyday sorts of situations?

Reflect: Joy happens; but it's also true that whatever we bring to a situation may affect how we—and others—experience it. Let's consider how joy might become something we do—how we might "en-joy" a situation—rather than something we simply experience passively. Take a moment to reflect on the three questions that follow and list what you notice about your own and others' experiences of joy.

- In the stories we've just heard, what kinds of attitudes or feelings "facilitated" joy?
- What was the context or environment for the experience of joy?
- How were these situations "en-joyed"; that is, how was joy brought or introduced into the situation by the participants themselves?

Connect: Joy is considered by many spiritual traditions, including Christianity, to be a mark of the presence of the Divine. Reflect on stories from your own spiritual tradition—from sacred writing or stories of holy people:

- Can you recall a story or saying from your spiritual tradition that reflects joy?
- What do you notice about joyful situations and people in these stories of joy? How do the people contribute to the joy making?
- What help do these traditions offer regarding joy and how to experience it more fully?
- How does this spiritual wisdom relate to what we've been discovering about joy in our own experiences?

Respond: We may not think of joy in connection with our work situations. Perhaps *satisfaction* and *achievement* are words that spring to mind more readily in connection with workplace fulfillment. We may be missing something, though, if we limit workplace joy to these kinds of experiences.

- How, when, where, or with whom do you experience joy at work?
- What kinds of things might you do to enjoy (i.e., experience joy) and "en-joy" (i.e., facilitate joy) your work and workplace more fully?

Bless: Offer the person on your left a word of hope or blessing for the coming week.

II: Fear—Can we make it creative?

Center: Let yourself relax for a moment, breathing deeply and reflecting on the fact that you are in the presence of Divine Mystery. Let pass before you any memorable moments—highs or lows—from your day or week so far; as they pass, listen to these words from Psalm 139 on page 72.

Check in: Can you share something about an action step you've been working on recently? Or say what work-related concern is most on your mind at the moment?

Focus: Today we continue our conversation on emotions at work with a look at fear. As children, we could deal with fear more easily if we were lucky enough to be with caring adults who were sensitive to our fears. As adults, however, we may find it difficult to deal with the fears within us. The prevalence of job-related anxiety and fears, particularly, is often the subject of public and private conversation. Let's begin by sharing our own experiences of fear.
- Can you recall a time when you were afraid as a child? What helped calm your fears?
- What personal fears do you encounter in your workplace, among colleagues, subordinates, and superiors, and within yourself?
- What are the corporate or institutional fears of your profession or organization?

Reflect: In his book, *The Care of the Soul,* Thomas Moore suggests that caring for the soul involves a special sort of attention to those emotions we often label "negative" (anger, jealousy, envy, fear, etc.). He maintains that these emotions hold a message from the soul that we need to hear if we are to honor and nurture our deepest selves. To ignore fear, to repress it, or even to "cure" it, without first listening to what it has to say, is to waste an opportunity to hear the voice of holy Spirit within. Perhaps, our fear alerts us to the fact that something our soul values is endangered in some way. Let's take a few moments to reflect on the fears—personal and corporate—we've noticed in our own workplaces:
- In the fears we articulated above, what of value is threatened?
- What deeper meaning do you sense in some of the workplace fears you've noticed?

Connect: Many spiritual traditions address the phenomenon of fear, offering their wisdom about how to relate creatively to this universal experience. In the Hebrew scriptures, for example, reluctant prophets are promised the continued presence of God and in Christian scriptures, the risen Christ says immediately to his disciples, "Fear not, it is I...." Cultural wisdom, too, speaks to our fearfulness.

- What spiritual wisdom from your own tradition has been especially helpful in dealing with work-related fears?
- What has your experience—or the experience of others—taught you about creative ways to deal with fear and the "message from the soul" it holds?

Respond: An active decision often does much to dispel fear. Let's consider what decisions we might make with respect to fear in the workplace:

- How might you incorporate some spiritual wisdom concerning fear into your daily life?
- What is one thing you might do to respond creatively to the deeper meaning contained in some fear you've noticed in your own workplace?

Bless: Offer the person on your left a word of hope or blessing for the coming week.

Psalm 139[1]

Lord, you have searched me out and known me.

You know my sitting down and my rising up; you discern my thoughts from afar.

You trace my journeys and my resting-places and are acquainted with all my ways.

Indeed, there is not a word on my lips, but you, O Lord, know it altogether.

You press upon me behind and before and lay your hand upon me.

Such knowledge is too wonderful for me; it is so high that I cannot attain to it.

Where can I go then from your Spirit? Where can I flee from your presence?

If I climb up to heaven, you are there; if I make the grave my bed, you are there also.

If I take the wings of the morning and dwell in the uttermost parts of the sea

Even there your hand will lead me and your right hand hold me fast.

If I say, "Surely the darkness will cover me, and the light around me turn to night,"

Darkness is not dark to you; the night is as bright as the day; darkness and light to you are both alike.

For you yourself created my inmost parts; you knit me together in my mother's womb.

I will thank you because I am marvelously made; your works are wonderful, and I know it well.

My body was not hidden from you, while I was being made in secret and woven in the depths of the earth.

Your eyes beheld my limbs, yet unfinished in the womb; all of them were written in your book; they were fashioned day by day, when as yet there was none of them. . . .

Search me out, O God and know my heart; try me and know my restless thoughts.

Look well whether there be any wickedness in me and lead me in the way that is everlasting.

Note

1. Translation from the Book of Common Prayer according to the use of The Episcopal Church (New York: Church Hymnal Corporation, 1979), 794, 795.

III: Surprise—How do we deal with the unexpected?

Center: Let yourself relax for a moment, breathing deeply and reflecting on the fact that you are in the presence of divine Mystery. Recall some moment of satisfaction—large or small—you experienced today. Let yourself dwell for a moment in the simple joy of that moment. Let that joy become a sort of light, infusing you and your day. As you recall the rest of your day, let it move with you from one place to another until you arrive at this time and place. When you've arrived here and are ready, open your eyes.

Check in: Can you share something about a recent action step or a work-related concern?

Focus: Whether we're at home or at work, emotions are part of who we are, part of our "standard equipment" as human beings. Finding skillful ways to honor our emotions can make us more effective. Conversely, the failure to honor them appropriately can create unnecessary crisis. Surprise is an emotion that we can experience as pleasant or unpleasant, depending on what evokes it. Recall your own experiences of feeling surprised, especially at work.

■ What occasioned your surprise?
■ Was yours a life-giving or life-draining surprise? What made it so?
■ How satisfied did you feel with the way you handled the unexpected?

Reflect: On page 75 is a true story of how one woman dealt creatively with an unexpected and unpleasant situation, surprising someone else in the process. After reading it, reflect on the way each character was surprised and the effect of the unexpected on each.

■ What made the experience of surprise life-giving for each character?
■ Do you know other stories of creative, life-giving responses to the unexpected?
■ Can you recall anything from your own spiritual tradition that speaks to handling the unexpected gracefully?

Connect: The unexpected can act as a sort of "wake-up call." If we're open to it, it can become a "crack" through which the Holy can touch and even heal us. It can initiate spiritual growth. Consider stories of "surprises" from your own spiritual tradition; find an example from the Christian scriptures on page 75 of this agenda.

■ Can you recall a time when you were surprised by divine Mystery?
■ What attitudes toward the unexpected might we cultivate to make a creative response to life's surprises more likely?
■ What aspects of a situation might facilitate creative response to the unexpected?
■ What spiritual resources or skills might be useful in dealing with the unexpected?

Respond: Surprise, by definition, is not something for which we can prepare, and yet conscious reflection on our experiences of surprise might predispose us to receive the unexpected in life-giving ways. Here are some possibilities:

1. Explore a spiritual practice this week that might open you more fully to divine surprises.
2. List recent surprises and your reactions to them, whether creative or not so creative; notice any patterns and reflect prayerfully on these.
3. Plan a pleasant surprise for someone with whom you work.

How else might you become more aware of the creative role of surprise in your life? In what other ways might you apply the insights of today's conversation to your life or work?

Bless: Offer the person on your left a word of hope or blessing for the coming week.

Two Tales of Surprise

From *Don't Forgive Too Soon: Extending the Two Hands That Heal*[1]

An elderly woman was accosted by a young man in his mid-twenties. The man, roughly pushing her backward, demanded her money. The woman quickly regained her balance and, pulling herself squarely up to her full height of 5'2", said in a firm voice devoid of accusation or pity, "Young man, what would your mother feel like if she knew you were doing this?"

The young man was so taken aback that he just stood for a moment in silence. Then in a half-embarrassed voice, he replied, "She'd be real hurt, real disappointed, ma'am."

"I know you'd never want that to happen and neither would I," said the woman as she walked by the young man with a smile and a nod.

From the Christian scriptures (Luke 24: 36–39, 45)

While [the disciples] were talking about [the reports of Jesus' appearance after his death], Jesus himself stood among them and said to them, "Peace be with you." They were startled and terrified and thought they were seeing a ghost. He said to them, "Why are you frightened, and why do doubts arise in your hearts. . . . Touch me and see; for a ghost does not have flesh and bones as you see I have." . . . Then he opened their minds to understand the scriptures.

Note

1. Sheila Fabricant Dennis and Matthew Linn, *Don't Forgive Too Soon: Extending the Two Hands That Heal* (New York: Paulist Press, 1997), 13.

IV: Anger—Can it be a spiritual discipline?

Center: Let yourself relax for a moment; breathe deeply and reflect on the fact that you are in the presence of divine Mystery. Recall some moment of satisfaction—large or small—you experienced today. Let yourself dwell for a moment in the simple joy of that moment. Let that joy become a sort of light, infusing you and your day. As you recall the rest of your day, let it move with you from one place to another until you arrive at this time and place. When you've arrived here and are ready, open your eyes.

Check in: Can you share something about an action step you've been working on recently? Or can you share what's been most life-giving or life-draining at work this week?

Focus: Concluding our series on emotion at work, we turn this week to anger. Mindful of ways anger can be destructive, many people are uncomfortable with this emotion, both their own and other people's. Our intent today is to seek ways to understand anger as a resource for spiritual growth. To introduce our conversation, let's begin by looking at our own experience with anger, past and present:
- What messages did you get as you were growing up about being angry and expressing your anger?
- How would you complete this sentence: "One thing that really pushes my buttons at work is . . ."

Reflect/Connect: In our conversation about fear, we reflected on Thomas Moore's assertion in his book *The Care of the Soul* that caring for the soul involves attending to so-called "negative" emotions such as anger and fear. Moore suggests that these emotions can teach us about ourselves in important ways. To suppress anger, or even to "heal" it, without first hearing what it has to teach, is to miss the voice of Spirit within us. But, of course, this begs the questions: "How are we to 'hear' our anger creatively? Can anger *really* become a spiritual discipline?" On page 77 is an exercise designed to help us "hear" the message of our anger. Let's take 20 minutes now to try it.
- What was the hardest thing about this exercise for you?
- What was most helpful or healing for you?
- Do you have a sense of any "message from the soul" in your anger?
- What did you learn from this exercise about yourself, your needs, or your values?

Respond: Most spiritual disciplines invite a creative, active response. Sometimes, using active imagination as a spiritual exercise can inspire an insight or course of action that had not occurred to us before. In other instances, such an exercise simply makes us more mindful of a part of our souls we might be tempted to neglect. Here are some possible action steps you might consider in response to today's experience:

1. Find references to anger in the writings of your own spiritual tradition. (Those using the Hebrew and Christian scriptures, for example, might look up *anger* and *angry* in a Bible concordance to locate such references.)
2. Continue the Honoring Anger meditation we did today until you reach a point of closure or until you see what you need to do in order to reach such a point.
3. Use other media (such as drawing, movement, working with clay) to express feelings you may have rediscovered today.
4. Create an action plan for dealing spiritually with anger in the future.

What creative and active response might you make to today's conversation?

Bless: Offer the person on your left a word of hope or blessing for the coming week.

Honoring Anger as a Spiritual Discipline[1]

Read through the steps of the exercise quickly before you begin. You won't be asked to read anything you have written to the group (although, of course, you are welcome to share whatever you'd like).

1. Close your eyes, and imagine you're with someone who is unconditionally supportive of you; perhaps a mentor, a close friend or relative—living or dead. And/or, recalling that you are surrounded by divine Presence, imagine the Divine present with you as Father or Mother or Friend.
2. Now, in your imagination, return to a time when you felt really angry at someone or about some situation at work, a person or situation about which you still have some concern. Let yourself feel again all the feelings that come over you: the frustration, anger, disappointment, hurt, fear, whatever.
3. As you experience these feelings, share them with that supportive friend who joined you in your imagination at the beginning of this exercise.

4. You may want to: a) write a letter to this person; b) write a dialogue between you and your friend in which you say both what you feel and what you need in this situation (use the present tense as you write); or c) visualize yourself sitting with your friend having a conversation.

5. Pay attention to how the friend responds to you. If you've written a letter, let the friend write back to you. Let the friend "speak" for your anger, telling you what message the anger wants you and others to hear.

6. Sit quietly for a few moments and breathe deeply as though you are breathing in the light and love of the divine Love.

Note

1. This exercise is based on a similar exercise, "Healing Process to Move Through Anger," found in *Don't Forgive Too Soon: Extending the Two Hands That Heal* by Dennis, Sheila Fabricant, and Matthew Linn (New York: Paulist Press, 1997), 50.

the divine at work

I: Making workspace sacred[1]

Center: Take a moment to reflect silently on your day, and give thanks for the presence of the Divine in it. Reflect briefly on your work environment: are there things in your workspace that remind you of the Divine there? In your imagination, dwell with these things briefly, giving thanks for them.

Check in: What can you share about a recent action step or about a work-related concern?

Focus: The faithful of many of the world's spiritual traditions have developed ways of making space sacred and of using space to remind them of the presence of the Holy. Hebrew and Christian scriptures, for example, contain numerous stories that suggest altars were built to give thanks, to mark key life transitions, and/or to recall encounters with the Divine:

> Then God said to Noah, "Go out of the ark, you and your wife, and your sons and your sons' wives with you. . . . So Noah went out with his sons and his wife and his sons' wives. . . . Then Noah built an altar to the Lord.
> —Genesis 8:15–16, 18, 20

Then the Lord appeared to Abram, and said, "To your offspring I will give this land." So he built there an altar to the Lord, who had appeared to him.

—Genesis 12:7

And that very night the Lord appeared to [Isaac] and said, "I am the God of your father Abraham; do not be afraid, for I am with you and will bless you and make your offspring numerous for my servant Abraham's sake." So he built an altar there, called on the name of the Lord, and pitched his tent there.

—Genesis 26:24–25

Of course, "workplace altars" may not look "religious" at all, but serve nonetheless to remind you of what's most important to you.

- Can you recall a time when something especially meaningful happened at work—when you "came close to the Holy" as it were—perhaps in a difficult situation, through the kindness of a colleague, or in some other way?
- What did you do to remind yourself of this important moment? Did you "build an altar" of some sort to mark the occasion? Why or why not?
- What other "altars" in your work space remind you of your deepest values?

Reflect: "Altar building" as we've been considering it may or may not be supported in your workplace. It might be useful to look at some values or attitudes that underlie what happens at work to see why we do or do not feel comfortable "building altars" there.

- What values present in your workplace support altar building and what values discourage it?
- What assumptions underlie these values or attitudes? (For example, an attitude might be: "Spirituality is private;" and the underlying assumption might be: "Private lives don't belong at work.")

Connect/Respond: While it may not occur to us to make our workspace "sacred" by building an "altar," few of us would argue about the importance of finding meaning in work or of staying true at work to that which we most value.

- Of what from your own spiritual tradition would you like to be reminded at work?
- For what might you want to give thanks?

- What might you take to work to give yourself a sense of the deeper meaning in your work?
- How might you construct your own "workplace altar" in a way that would be both appropriate to your work setting and meaningful to you?
- How else might you apply the insights from today's conversation in your own work context?

Bless: Share a one- or two-word blessing with the person on your left.

II: Rituals that work at work

Center: Use a sacred word or phrase from your own spiritual tradition to center yourself. Say the word or phrase silently to yourself as you inhale and as you exhale, becoming aware that you are in the presence of divine Mystery.

Check in: Can your share something of either a recent action step or a work-related concern?

Focus: We've begun a series of conversations focused on the Divine at work. This week we consider simple actions, or rituals, that we can use to frame time, just as altars help sanctify space. While we tend to associate "ritual" with religious or spiritual actions, rituals can serve many functions. Let's look at the idea of ritual in a more general sense:

- How do you make the transition between home and work in the morning and evening?
- What work routines are especially satisfying to you?
- Do you begin or end each work day in any specific ways?
- What sorts of things do you find it hardest to let go of at work?

Reflect: Personal rituals can assist us with transitions, remind us of or connect us to things we value, and/or focus our attention on deeper meaning present in our actions. Not all daily rituals are spiritual, of course, but rituals that help us integrate our spirituality into our daily lives may deepen the meaning of our work.

- Where do you find meaning in your work? What actions do you take to remind yourself of this meaning?
- What do you do at work to remind yourself of the things you most value?

Connect: The desire to integrate spirituality and work seems to be an increasing concern of our own culture. In some cultures, present and past, spirituality and work are not seen as separate; rather, spirituality is simply an ordinary part of the way work is done. Below are examples of work-related rituals: two prayers from an ancient culture and some suggestions from a contemporary source. Look them over and see how they resonate with your own needs and experience.

- What are your own thoughts about the place of ritual in work life?
- What function does/could it appropriately play at work?
- What elements would a prayer for your own workday include?

Respond: Becoming more aware of the place and value of work-related ritual can make the workday a richer experience.

- Is there some work-related ritual with which you'd be willing to experiment in the coming week?
- What other action step could you take in response to today's conversation?
- How else might you apply the insights of today's conversation to your own life?

Bless: Offer the person on your left a word of hope or blessing for the coming week.

Rituals for Work

Two Prayers of Celtic Farmers[2]

> I will go out to sow the seed,
> In name of Him who gave it growth . . .
> Should a grain fall on bare rock,
> It shall have no soil in which to grow;
> As much as falls into the earth,
> The dew will make it to be full. . . .
>
> God bless Thou Thyself my reaping,
> Each ridge, and plain, and field,
> Each sickle curved, shapely hard,
> Each ear and handful in the sheaf . . .
> Surround Thou the flocks and herds.
> Tend them to a kindly fold.

From a Forwarded E-mail, Source Unspecified

Most of us are working harder and longer hours, and find it difficult to just "let go" at the end of the workday. You're still thinking of that project that needs to be completed, the meeting tomorrow, those phone calls you didn't get to. Subsequently, your down time at home with the family may suffer. And yet psychologists note that time with family is crucial to a satisfying life. Here are a few ideas on how to "turn it off" at the end of the workday and reconnect with your private life:

- Use the last 15 minutes of the workday to do low-pressure tasks. Clean off your desk, return one or two calls to people you enjoy dealing with. More importantly, take the time to plan and write down tomorrow's tasks. Trying to remember them will just keep your mind preoccupied all night.
- Make a point of noticing the scenery on your journey home. Smell the air, notice the trees or the sky. It will help distance you from the workday, relax you and remind you of a larger perspective.
- When you get home, don't immediately launch into a litany about how tough your day was. Ask your family to also hold off on their demands for a few minutes to a half an hour. Use this time to change clothes, take a shower or a walk, enjoy a cup of tea or a glass of wine.
- Establish rituals. Simple things like family dinners have gotten lost in today's busy lifestyle. Try to create "touchstones" at home that make you all reconnect. This can be sitting down once a week to a meal together, spending an evening together watching a certain show on TV, etc. If you tend to be a workaholic—and these days, it's difficult to avoid overworking yourself—remember the big picture. Someone once said that, as we lie on our deathbeds, most of us probably won't wish we'd worked harder.

Note

1. My thanks to Pat Sullivan whose thoughts about workplace altars inspired this agenda.

2. Esther de Waal, ed., *The Celtic Vision: Selections from the Carmina Gadelica* (Petersham, Massachusetts: St. Bedes's Publications, 1990), 51, 53.

III: Meaning and leadership

Center: Breathe deeply, relaxing any tension you may discover in your body. Closing your eyes if you wish, reflect on the fact that you and your situation are part of a much larger picture and that even this "larger picture" is contained within divine Love. As you breathe in, imagine yourself taking in that Love; as you breathe out, let go for the moment of any lesser matters or anxieties.

Check in: Can you share something of either a recent action step or a work-related concern?

Focus: One remarkable aspect of a natural system is its ability to maintain its basic shape and organization even though its parts are in constant flux; its organization is "globally stable [and] locally changing."[1] The human body is an example of this: individual cells die and are replaced, but the system as a whole remains healthy. In her book, *Leadership and the New Science: Learning About Organizations from an Orderly Universe,* Meg Wheatley suggests that successful human organizations, such as corporations, share this characteristic ability to balance stability and change. A key to maintaining this balance, she believes, is meaning: the values of the organization, those leading it, and those working in it. The excerpt on page 85 summarizes her understanding. As you read it, note any resonance with your own experience.

- Where do you see evidence of the meaning or values of your own workplace? Can you give an example?
- What role does meaning play in your experience of work?
- Can you summarize the guiding vision, values, or meaning that seem to underlie the actual day-to-day operating of your organization's leadership, or of your own work team, office, or profession?
- What operating assumptions that are at play in your own work team or profession either support or contradict the perspective expressed in the Wheatley excerpt?

Reflect/Connect: Compare Wheatley's understanding with the wisdom of the Tao Te Ching[2] in a modern paraphrase:

> Being centered means having the ability to recover one's balance, even in the midst of actions. A centered person is not subject to passing whims or sudden excitements. Being grounded means being down-to-earth, having gravity or weight. I know where I stand, and I know what I stand for.
> —#26 Tao Te Ching

The leader knows that constant interventions will block the group's process. The leader does not insist that things come out a certain way.

—#2 Tao Te Ching

The leader follows the group's lead and is open to whatever emerges. . . . Being open and attentive is more effective than being judgmental. This is because people naturally tend to be good and truthful when they are being received in a good and truthful manner.

—#49 Tao Te Ching

- What anecdote, image, or memory comes to mind as you reflect on these sayings?
- What texts or insights from your own spiritual tradition seem to relate here?
- How do these sayings relate to Wheatley's observations?

Respond: Let's reflect on what we're seeing and how these insights might apply in our own work situation or organization:

- How do the insights that we've generated today relate to your own work?
- Especially in those areas in which you offer leadership, how might you become more aware of the values underlying your own work?
- How might you assist your organization or work team to become more aware of the meaning inherent in the work of the organization?

Bless: Offer the person on your left a word of hope or blessing for the coming week.

From *Leadership and the New Science,* by Margaret J. Wheatley[3]

The very best organizations have a fractal [self-similar] quality to them. An observer of such an organization can tell what the organization's values and ways of doing business are by watching anyone, whether it be a production floor employee or a senior manager. There is a consistency and predictability to the quality of behavior. No matter where we look in these organizations, self-similarity is found in its people, in spite of the complex range and levels.

How is the quality achieved? The potent force that shapes behavior in these . . . organizations, as in all natural systems, is the combination of simply expressed expectations of acceptable behavior and the freedom available to individuals to assert themselves . . . [Such] organizations . . .

have learned to trust in . . . the power of guiding principles or values, knowing that they are strong enough influences of behavior to shape every employee into a desired representative of the organization. These organizations expect to see similar behaviors show up at every level in the organization because those behaviors were patterned into the organizing principles at the very start.

[In biological systems . . .] the structure is capable of maintaining its overall shape and a large degree of independence from the environment because each part of the system is free to express itself within the context of that system. Fluctuations, randomness, and unpredictability at the local level, in the presence of guiding or self-referential principles, cohere over time into definite and predictable form. . . .

These ideas speak with a simple clarity to issues of effective leadership. They bring us back to the importance of simple governing principles: guiding visions, strong values, organizational beliefs—the few rules individuals can use to shape their own behavior. The leader's task is to communicate them, to keep them ever-present and clear, and then allow individuals in the system their random, sometimes chaotic-looking meanderings.

This is no simple task. Anytime we see systems in apparent chaos, our training urges us to interfere, to stabilize and shore things up. But if we can trust the workings of chaos, we will see that the dominant shape of our organizations can be maintained if we retain clarity about the purpose and direction of the organization. If we succeed in maintaining focus, rather than hands-on control, we also create the flexibility and responsiveness that every organization craves. What leaders are called upon to do in a chaotic world is to shape their organizations through concepts, not through elaborate rules or structures.

Ever since my imagination was captured by the phrase "strange attractor"[4] I have wondered if we could identify such a force in organizations . . . a force so attractive that it pulls all behavior toward it, [creating] coherence. My current belief is that we do have such attractors at work in organizations and . . . one of [these] is meaning . . .

I became aware of the call of meaning in our organizational lives when I worked with a number of incoherent companies that had been tipped into chaos by reorganizations or leveraged buy outs. They had lost any purpose beyond the basic struggle to survive. Yet under these circumstances I saw some employees who continued to work hard and contribute. . . even when the organization could offer them nothing. . . . it became evident that [these employees] had taken the time to create a meaning for their work, one that transcended present organizational circumstances. . . . They held onto personal coherence because of the meaning attractor they created. Maybe the organization didn't make sense, but their lives did.

I have also seen companies make deliberate use of meaning to move through times of traumatic change . . . leaders mak[ing] great efforts to speak forthrightly and frequently to employees about current struggles, about the tough times that lie ahead, and about their dream[s] of the future. These conversations fill a painful period with new purpose.... In most cases, given this kind of meaningful information, workers respond with allegiance and energy....We instinctively reach out to leaders who work with us on creating meaning. Those who give voice and form to our search for meaning, and who help us make our work purposeful, are leaders we cherish ... When a meaning attractor is in place in an organization, employees can be trusted to move freely, drawn in many directions by their energy and creativity.

Notes

1. Margaret Wheatley, *Leadership and the New Science: Learning about Organizations from an Orderly Universe* (San Francisco: Berrett-Koehler, 1994), 132.

2. John Heider, *The Tao of Leadership: Lao Tzu's Tao Te Ching Adapted for a New Age* (Atlanta: Humanics New Age, 1985), 51, 3, 97, respectively.

3. Margaret Wheatley, *Leadership and the New Science: Learning About Organizations from an Orderly Universe* (San Francisco: Berrett-Koehler, 1994), 132–35.

4. *Strange attractor* is a scientific term for a pattern generated over time when the process of a changing natural system is plotted mathematically. The shape thus generated expresses the limits outside of which the process of the system will not take it. Although the process may seem chaotic and unpredictable, its strange attractor reveals an order inherent in both the process and the system. It's as though the process is "attracted" to this order; the "attractor" is a sort of "force" compelling order.

IV: Trusting divine Wholeness at work

Center: Breathe deeply several times and relax any physical tension you may be experiencing. Let yourself simply *be still*. You may be aware of the pressures of the day, but these don't touch the core of stillness deep within you. This stillness is divine Mystery, present around and within you. Let yourself rest in this Mystery.

Check in: Can you share something of either a recent action step or a work-related concern?

Focus: Many of us find that although we want to believe and trust in a deeper wholeness, we often struggle with anxiety and uncertainty as we experience stress at work and elsewhere. Some of this stress may result from outer pressures at work; some of it may be self-generated anxiety.

Perhaps by stepping back and looking at both our experience of stress at work and our longing for a more creative alternative, we can discover ways to move toward the wholeness we know is present.

- What is your own experience of stress-at-work issues?
- How do you experience the interplay of outer, work-related pressure and inner, self-generated stress?
- What three words would you use to describe your own longing for deeper wholeness or a more creative alternative to work/life stress?

Reflect: Frederick Buechner writes of a time in his life when he was deeply stressed and fearful. Take a moment now to read the Reflect section on page 89. The word often used for this sort of experience is *synchronicity,* a seemingly coincidental occurrence in which some outer event seems to speak directly to an inner need. Some people feel that synchronistic events suggest a deeper wholeness inherent in the cosmos.

- Have you—or someone you know—ever had an experience of synchronicity?
- How might the occasions of stress you experience in your life hide an invitation to trust more deeply?
- Can you recall a time when life circumstances seemed to invite a deeper trust? How did you respond?
- What current work-related concern might be inviting this sort of trust?

Connect/Respond: Reflected in the writings of many spiritual traditions are both the assumption that divine Wholeness can be trusted and the assumption that human beings will need to be reassured of this fact! A couple of examples of these are found in the "Connect and Respond" section on page 89.

- What texts from the writings of your own tradition come to mind in this connection?
- What sorts of things reassure you of a deeper Wholeness present in your life?
- Are there spiritual disciplines you use to remind yourself to trust this deeper Wholeness?
- What action might you take to stay more aware of the presence of the Divine in your life and work?

Bless: Offer the person on your left a word of hope or blessing for the coming week.

Read and Reflect

I remember sitting parked by the roadside once, terribly depressed and afraid about my daughter's illness and what was going on in our family, when out of nowhere a car came along down the highway with a license plate that bore on it the one word out of all the words in the dictionary that I needed most to see exactly then. The word was TRUST. What do you call a moment like that? Something to laugh off as the kind of joke life plays on us every once in a while? The word of God? I am willing to believe that maybe it was something of both, but for me it was an epiphany. The owner of the car turned out to be, as I'd suspected, a trust officer in a bank, and not long ago having read an account I wrote of the incident somewhere, he found out where I lived and one afternoon brought me the license plate itself, which sits propped up on a bookshelf in my house to this day. It is rusty around the edges and a little battered, and it is also as holy a relic as I have ever seen.

—Frederick Buechner in Telling Secrets[1]

Read, Connect, and Respond

Do not be afraid, little flock, for it is your Father's good pleasure to give you the kingdom. Sell your possessions, and give alms. Make purses for yourselves that do not wear out, an unfailing treasure in heaven where no thief comes near and no moth destroys. For where your treasure is, there your heart will be also.

—Christian scriptures, Luke 12:32–34

When I let go of what I am, I become what I might be. When I let go of what I have, I receive what I need.

These are the feminine or Yin paradoxes:
- By yielding, I endure.
- The empty space is filled.
- When I give of myself, I become more.
- When I feel most destroyed, I am about to grow.
- When I desire nothing, a great deal comes to me.

Have you ever struggled to get work or love and finally given up and found both love and work were suddenly there?

Do you want to be free and independent? Conform to God's law; that is how everything happens anyway.

When I give up trying to impress the group, I become very impressive. But when I am just trying to make myself look good, the group knows that and does not like it.

My best work is done when I forget my own point of view; the less I make of myself, the more I am.

When I yield to the wishes of the person working, I encounter no resistance. . . .

—#22 Tao Te Ching

Notes

1. Frederick Buechner, *Telling Secrets: A Memoir* (San Francisco: HarperSanFrancisco, 1991), 49–50.

2. John Heider, *The Tao of Leadership: Lao Tzu's Tao Te Ching Adapted for a New Age* (Atlanta: Humanics New Age, 1985), 43.

reflecting with the tao

I: Being oneself

Center: Take a moment to relax and breathe deeply, closing your eyes if you wish. You are invited to enjoy the hospitality of divine Mystery, the Presence of the "beginning and the end," of the One who simply Is. Rest in the timelessness of this present moment. Remain in this present as you return to the group and our conversation.

Check in: Can you share something of a recent action step or a work-related concern on your mind at the moment?

Focus/Reflect: Today we begin a four-session exploration of a Chinese spiritual classic, the *Tao Te Ching,* seeking ways to apply its wisdom to our own work situation and to bring it into dialogue with our own spiritual traditions. Written in the fifth century BCE, the *Tao Te Ching* (pronounced "dow du jing") presents the reflections of sage Lao Tzu on the nature of reality. Its title means *The Book of How Things Happen or Work.* Let's begin by reading an excerpt from a modern paraphrase of the *Tao* (on page 93) about the importance of being centered.

- Can you recall a time at work—or elsewhere—when you felt especially centered?

- Can you think of a colleague or mentor, current or past, who seems to you especially centered?
- How would you characterize being centered or grounded? Can you suggest an image or some adjectives that capture the sense of what being grounded means for you?
- Have you noticed what effect being centered has on others in a work situation? Have you noticed the effects of a leader's *failing* to be centered on those with whom s/he works?

Connect: Lao Tzu suggests that being grounded means knowing where you stand, knowing what you stand for. He also suggests that the grounded leader has a sense of self.

- In your experiences of being centered, what did you stand for?
- In what situations do you most often have a sense of self?
- What stories or sayings from your own spiritual tradition come to mind as you reflect on these passages?
- Are there sages or saints from your spiritual tradition who you'd characterize as centered, who have a sense of self? What made (makes) them so?

Respond: Few would argue with the thought that moving toward being centered or coming to a deeper sense of oneself is a good thing. We might wonder, however, just how to begin this movement. Here are some ways we might experiment in the coming weeks:

1. Pay special attention to times at work when you feel you are especially centered. Reflect on what contributes to this centered-ness.
2. In situations of tension or conflict, notice who, if anyone, is centered.
3. Spend a few minutes at your desk each morning experimenting with "centering exercises" you might know; you could use one or more of the centering exercises that begin our conversation agenda.
4. Make a list of qualities you feel are important aspects of your "self" and beside them note situations at work in which you might express these aspects.

Is there one of these you might be willing to try this week? Can you think of another sort of "action step" that might facilitate your becoming more centered or grounded at work?

Bless: Offer the person on your left a word of hope or blessing for the coming week.

From John Heider's
The Tao of Leadership[1] #26: Center and Ground

The leader who is centered and grounded can work with erratic people and critical group situations without harm.

Being centered means having the ability to recover one's balance, even in the midst of actions. A centered person is not subject to passing whims or sudden excitements.

Being grounded means being down-to-earth, having gravity or weight. I know where I stand, and I know what I stand for: that is ground.

The centered and grounded leader has stability and a sense of self. . . .

Note

1. John Heider, *The Tao of Leadership: Lao Tzu's Tao Te Ching Adapted for a New Age* (Atlanta: Humanics New Age, 1985), 51.

II: *Polarities and paradoxes*

Center: Take a moment to relax and breathe deeply, closing your eyes if you wish. You are invited to enjoy the hospitality of divine Mystery, the Presence of "the beginning and the end," of the One who simply Is. Rest in the timelessness of this present moment. Remain in this present as you return to the group and our conversation.

Check in: Can you share something about the action step you chose as a result of a recent conversation? Or, can you share something about the work-related issue or concern most on your mind at the moment?

Focus: Today we continue to focus our conversation on the ancient Chinese spiritual classic, the *Tao Te Ching*. We look at the paradoxical nature of leadership, reflecting on the *Tao's* insight that polarities seem to be part of our reality. Let's look first at the excerpt from *The Tao of Leadership* on page 95.

- Can you recall experiences, perhaps work-related, that demonstrate the truth of any of these insights from the *Tao?*
- Have you known "wise leaders" who led in any of the ways suggested?
- Have you discovered through experience the wisdom of these ways of leading?

■ Can you remember an occasion when such leadership might have been helpful but wasn't employed?

Reflect/Connect: Polarities and paradoxes seem to be a part of the wisdom of many spiritual traditions. Many of the sayings and stories of Jesus, for example, seem to suggest such polarities or contain paradoxes (for instance, "those who want to save their life will lose it," Mark 8:35).

■ What wisdom from your own spiritual tradition contains paradox or suggests polarity?

■ In what ways does this wisdom speak to your own professional practice? Can you cite some examples?

■ How does the wisdom of your own spiritual tradition or of the *Tao Te Ching* contrast with what we might call the "conventional wisdom" of your workplace or professional culture?

Respond: Reflection is certainly a good place to start, but to become wise leaders, we must move beyond reflection to action. Even simple decisions to act may make a difference. Here are a few ways we might begin:

1. Identify some area in which your behavior at work tends to be "over-determined." Notice this behavior in action, keeping a journal of such instances for the week.
2. Do you have a relationship at work in which polarities tend to manifest? Decide on some action typical of a wise leader and experiment with it in this relationship.
3. During meetings this week, notice when "constant interventions block the group's process." If you are facilitating the meeting, experiment with non-intervention.
4. Select a passage from today's reading or from your own spiritual tradition, and as you make your way home after work each day, reflect on how it has or might have applied to your interactions during the day.

Is there one of these you might be willing to try this week? Can you think of some other action step that might be more appropriate for your own work context?

Bless: Offer the person on your left a word of hope or blessing for the coming week.

From John Heider's
The Tao of Leadership #2: Polarities[1]

All behavior consists of opposites or polarities. If I do anything more and more, over and over, its polarity will appear. For example, striving to be beautiful makes a person ugly, and trying too hard to be kind is a form of selfishness.

Any over-determined behavior produces its opposite:

- An obsession with living suggests worry about dying.
- True simplicity is not easy.
- Is it a long time or a short time since we last met?
- The braggart probably feels small and insecure.
- Who would be first ends up last.

Knowing how polarities work, the wise leader does not push to make things happen, but allows process to unfold on its own.

The leader teaches by example rather than by lecturing others on how they ought to be.

The leader knows that constant interventions will block the group's process. The leader does not insist that things come out in a certain way.

The wise leader does not seek a lot of money or a lot of praise. Nevertheless, there is plenty of both.

Note

1. John Heider, *The Tao of Leadership: Lao Tzu's Tao Te Ching Adapted for a New Age* (Atlanta: Humanics New Age, 1985), 3.

III: Success

Center: Take a moment to relax and breathe deeply, closing your eyes if you wish. You are invited to enjoy the hospitality of divine Mystery, the Presence of "the beginning and the end," of the One who simply Is. Rest in the timelessness of this present moment. Remain in this present as you return to the group and our conversation.

Check in: Can you share something about the action step you chose as a result of a recent conversation? Or can you share the things at work for which you are most and/or least thankful at the moment?

Focus: Success is something we all hope for, strive for, but it can be a mixed bag, both life-giving and life-draining. Recall for a moment your "most spectacular success": perhaps an experience from your childhood or youth, perhaps from your adult or work life.

- Can you share something of your success story?
- In what ways was the experience life-giving; in what ways life-draining?
- Can you recall any experience which you regarded as a success at the time but which you've come to look at differently as time has passed?

Reflect/Connect: Today we continue to use as our resource a Chinese spiritual classic, the *Tao Te Ching,* which says some interesting things about the tricky nature of success. Let's take a reflective look at the excerpt from the *Tao* on page 97. As you read, note anything that seems especially true in your experience; also note any questions the excerpt provokes in you.

- Which of the reflections from the excerpt seems especially true in your experience? Can you give examples?
- What questions do these reflections raise for you?
- What thoughts do you have about how we can creatively "live with the fruits of success"?
- What do you recall from the wisdom of your own spiritual tradition regarding success and how we might live with it creatively?
- How does your own spiritual tradition measure success?
- Are there ways to enjoy success and still care for yourself properly?

Respond: It's often useful to see how we might apply the insights of our conversations to our own specific work contexts. For example, you might:

1. Pay special attention this week to the ways those with whom you work respond to success. Are there any responses worth emulating; any to avoid?
2. As you make your way home from work each day, reflect on the day's successes, large and small; ask: how can I care for myself in relation to these successes?
3. Consider your "reputation." Reflect, maybe in writing, on ways you're tempted to "preserve it, [losing] the freedom and honesty necessary for further development."
4. Make a list of ways you might "foster success in other people," especially those with whom you work, and select one of these ways for immediate action.

Is there one of these—or some other action step—you'd like to try this week? How else might you apply the insights of today's conversation to your own work or work context?

Bless: Offer the person on your left a word of hope or blessing for the coming week.

From John Heider's
The Tao of Leadership #13: Success[1]

If you measure success in terms of praise and criticism, your anxiety will be endless.

Having a good reputation or becoming well known for your work can be a hindrance to your further development.

Fame is as burdensome as caring for yourself properly.

What is the problem with praise and criticism?

If the group applauds one thing you do, and then you feel good, you will worry if they do not applaud as loudly the next time. If they are critical, if they argue or complain, you will feel hurt. Either way, you are anxious and dependent.

How can a good reputation be a hindrance?

A good reputation naturally arises from doing good work. But if you try to cherish your reputation, if you try to preserve it, you lose the freedom and honesty necessary for further development.

How is fame like caring for yourself?

In order to do good work, you must take good care of yourself. You must value yourself and allow others to value you also. But if you make too much of yourself, you will become egocentric. Egocentricity injures both self and work.

If you can live with the fruits of success and care for yourself properly, you will be able to foster success in other people.

IV: Connecting spirituality and work

Center: Take a moment to relax and breathe deeply, closing your eyes if you wish. You are invited to enjoy the hospitality of divine Mystery, the Presence of the "beginning and the end," of the One who simply Is. Rest in the timelessness of this present moment. Remain in this present as you return to the group and our conversation.

Check in: Can you share something about the action step you chose as a result of a recent conversation? If you prefer, share a high or low point of your work week so far.

Focus/Reflect: Week by week we explore connections between our spirituality and our work. These connections take many forms depending on our work contexts, the various situations in which we find ourselves, and our own personal inclinations. Today we conclude our series on *The Tao of Leadership* by looking at several brief excerpts from the *Tao*, each of which presents a slightly different slant on spirituality at work. As you read over the excerpts beginning on page 99, be mindful of your own work experience: of colleagues with whom you have worked, of situations in which your own leadership was especially effective—or not; of your own vision for work. Take a moment to jot down these connections if you wish.

■ What people, experiences, anecdotes, images came to mind as you reflected on the excerpts?

■ What was your feeling reaction, positive or negative, to any of these?

■ Did any of these strike you as being particularly wise and true? Any seem really off base?

Connect: Reflect for a moment on the wisdom of your own spiritual tradition as you recall it. Do you find exemplified in the lives of its heroes and heroines any of the wisdom expressed in today's excerpts from the *Tao?*

■ Are there connections between the values or principles of your own spiritual tradition and the wisdom of the *Tao* as expressed in today's excerpts?

■ What questions occur to you regarding the practicality of this wisdom for today's world?

■ How might the wisdom of the *Tao* or your spiritual tradition look in your own work context?

Respond: Spirituality at work, of course, is as much about action as it is about conversation. Let's consider how we might apply the insights of today's conversation to our specific contexts. Here are some possibilities:

1. Select one of the excerpts from today's agenda, and make it the focus this week of a brief daily meditation.

2. Identify the quote that you found most compelling or most troubling, and pay special attention this week to situations at work to which it might apply.

3. Decide on one work-related behavior suggested to you by today's readings, and practice it with special intention this week.
4. At the end of each day, read over the excerpts again, recalling situations from your day that reflected each.

Is there one of these you might be willing to try this week? Or how else might you apply the insights of today's conversation to your own work situation?

Bless: Offer the person on your left a word of hope or blessing for the coming week.

From John Heider's
The Tao of Leadership [1]

#23, Be Still

The wise leader speaks rarely and briefly. After all, no other natural outpouring goes on and on. It rains and then it stops. It thunders and then it stops.

The leader teaches more through being than through doing. The quality of one's silence conveys more than long speeches.

Be still. Follow your inner wisdom. In order to know your inner wisdom, you have to be still.

The leader who knows how to be still and feel deeply will probably be effective. . . .

Tao works for those who follow Tao. God serves those who serve God. When you are in touch with the single principle, you can consciously cooperate with it. . . .

Remember the method is awareness-of-process. Reflect. Be still.

What do you deeply feel?

#49, Be Open to Whatever Emerges

The wise leader does not impose a personal agenda or value system on the group.

The leader follows the group's lead and is open to whatever emerges. . . .

Being open and attentive is more effective than being judgmental. This is because people naturally tend to be good and truthful when they are being received in a good and truthful manner.

. . . openness is simply more potent than any system of judgments ever devised.

#72, Spiritual Awareness

Group work must include spiritual awareness if it is to touch the existential anxiety of our times. Without awe, the awful remains unspoken; a diffuse malaise remains.

Be willing to speak of traditional religion, no matter how offended some group members may be. Overcome the bias against the word God. The great force of our spiritual roots lies in tradition, like it or not.

The wise leader models spiritual behavior and lives in harmony with spiritual values. There is a way of knowing, higher than reason; there is a self, greater than egocentricity.

Note

1. John Heider, *The Tao of Leadership: Lao Tzu's Tao Te Ching Adapted for a New Age* (Atlanta: Humanics New Age, 1985), 45, 97, 143, respectively.

soul at work

I: Valuing ourselves

Center: Take a deep breath and become aware of any tension in your body. Relax that tension and imagine you are being held in a circle of warm and healing Light. Relax as this Light "melts" the stresses of the day. Rest in the wholeness this Light is bringing you.

Check in: Can you share how a recent action step is going? Or say what about your work has been most life-giving and/or life-draining recently?

Focus: Today we begin a series of conversations exploring the ways our souls—our deepest selves—are tended, energized, and nourished in and through our work. Tending the soul at work can involve paying attention to our own value, noticing the "value added" we bring to our work places. Let's begin by considering the ways we know our own value, a knowledge that comes both from within and without.

- What are some ways you know when your work is of value?
- Can you recall a specific situation in which you experienced the work of another as especially valuable? How did you communicate this to the other?

■ What role does money play in the valuing process?
■ Can you recall a situation in which you were unsure about the value you were contributing to a project at work; how was this for you?

Reflect: While others can play an important role in helping us recognize the value we add to our work, our own self-valuing may be even more essential. This valuing is, in fact, a key aspect of healthy self-care. Consider for a moment how you communicate to yourself that your work has value.
■ What do you do to express self-appreciation?
■ How do you acknowledge to yourself that you—your work, your thoughts—are important?
■ What inhibitions do you have about self-valuing?

Connect: On page 103 are some stories from *The Artist's Way at Work: Riding the Dragon* by Mark Bryan, Julia Cameron, and Catherine Allen. These stories illustrate self-valuing and suggest that small acts of "luxury" can be a concrete way to acknowledge ourselves at work.
■ How does the idea of rewarding or acknowledging yourself at work strike you? What difference do you think it might make for you?
■ What do you know of having "a sense of personal continuity" or "personal passion"?
■ What wisdom from your spiritual tradition speaks to the importance of self-valuing?
■ Are there aspects of your spiritual tradition that seem to imply self-care is not wise?

Respond: Self-care at work is not especially difficult if we believe in its value and become intentional about its practice. Let's consider how we might respond to the insights of today's conversation. The authors of *The Artist's Way at Work* suggest making a list of simple ways we might practice self-care at work. Take a moment to list for yourself little "luxuries" you might give yourself or things you might do to express self-appreciation.
■ Can you share something from your list and suggest why you chose this?
■ How else might you apply the insights of today's conversation to your work life?

Bless: Offer the person on your left a word of hope or blessing for the coming week.

From *The Artist's Way at Work:*
Riding the Dragon by Mark Bryan,
Julia Cameron, and Catherine Allen[1]

... Jacob, a corporate lawyer, ... bought a refillable leather notebook with blank pages. Small enough to fit in his briefcase, it doubled as a sketch-pad/diary. He used it for random insights, quick doodles, the odd sketch grabbed when he was alone, at lunch, or waiting for a meeting to convene. "That little book gave me a sense of me—me before, during, and after my business life. It was a handsome book, I loved the feel of it, but I loved even more the feeling it gave me that my life and thoughts were personal and important."

William, a tough and bitter corporate warrior, began carrying disposable pocket cameras in his briefcase. At a business dinner or after a successful meeting he would take a shot or two. Printing the film, he would order duplicates. One set went on to a corkboard in his office. The other set was sent as thoughtful mementos to his colleagues. "The snaps took very little time and very little money, but they added up to my feeling that my life counted for something," he said.

For Alice, using nice note cards to write business thank-yous gave her a sense of luxury. For Carl, it was a good Waterman pen.

"I think luxury is having a sense of personal continuity, of personal passion, in the midst of a busy public life," Julia postulates.

Note

1. Mark Bryan, Julia Cameron, and Catherine Allen, *The Artist's Way at Work: Riding the Dragon* (New York: William Morrow and Company, Inc., 1998), 98–99.

II: *Creating community*

Center: Take a deep breath and become aware of any tension in your body. Relax that tension and imagine you are being held in a circle of warm and healing Light. Relax as this Light "melts" the stresses of the day. Rest in the wholeness this Light is bringing you.

Check in: If you wish, share something of your centering meditation, or share something of what you're most or least grateful for.

Focus: We sometimes experience our work lives as soul- or spirit-draining, but in their essay, "Spirited Connections: Learning to Tap the Spiritual Resources in Our Lives and Work," D. Susan Wisely and Elizabeth Lynn suggest that organizational life need not be hostile to the life of the soul; rather, since the workplace is a principal arena for connection to the larger world, it is a potential spiritual resource to contemporary culture:

> Our spirits are nurtured by *living in relation*—in relation to others and to a larger good. But our life in relation to others has been diminished by the structures of modern existence. . . . How can we help our own institutions . . . to yield that crucial sense of connection to others and to a larger creation?[1]

- Can you recall an occasion at work in which you have experienced a "sense of connection to others [and/or] a larger good"?
- What about the occasion or interchange facilitated this "sense of connection"?

Reflect: Wisely and Lynn have found that the telling of personal stories builds community in ways that more formal discussions often don't. They speculate that storytelling leads to a deeper sort of listening, in which the hearer suspends disbelief, listening with openness and without judgment. The teller, too, experiences a special freedom. Wisely and Lynn believe in the importance of "clearing hospitable spaces within our ordinary work situations, where we can enter into . . . conversation with our . . . colleagues. . . ."

- Does your own experience suggest that "storytelling" is useful in the work setting? Why or why not?
- In what sorts of situations is community in the workplace an asset?
- Can you envision ways in which such conversation might be introduced to creative effect in your work context?

Connect/Respond: Jürgen Moltmann, a contemporary Christian theologian, points to the Christian Trinitarian image of God—one God in three Persons—suggesting that the basic "unit" of divine Mystery is not individual but community: God is a Fellowship into which human beings are invited. Human community, facilitated by Spirit, mirrors and issues from this divine Community.[2]

- How does this concept of divine Mystery relate to our conversation so far?
- What do you recall from the wisdom of your own spiritual tradition about the nature of community?
- How might you facilitate "the creation of life-giving community" in your own workplace or profession?

Bless: As we close offer the person on your left a simple word of hope or blessing for the coming week.

Notes

1. D. Susan Wisely and Elizabeth Lynn, "Spirited Connections: Learning to Tap the Spiritual Resources in Our Lives and Work," in *Spirit at Work*, Jay A. Conger ed. (San Francisco: Jossey-Bass, 1994), 100.

2. Jürgen Moltmann, *The Spirit of Life: A Universal Affirmation* (Minneapolis: Fortress Press, 1992), 118, 119.

III: *Creativity revisited*

Center: Take a deep breath and become aware of any tension in your body. Relax that tension and imagine you are being held in a circle of warm and healing Light. Relax as this Light "melts" the stresses of the day. Rest in the wholeness this Light is bringing you.

Check in: Can you share something about an action step you chose as a result of a recent conversation? Or, say what has been most life-giving or life-draining about your work recently?

Focus: Today we consider the topic of creativity in work, looking at the connections between creativity and soul. *Creativity* means many things to many people, so let's begin by looking at our own understandings of the idea:

- What images come to your mind when you think of creativity?
- Reflecting on your childhood and youth, can you recall an occasion when you were especially creative?
- How would you define *creativity?*

Reflect/Connect: Author and psychologist Thomas Moore suggests in his *Care of the Soul* that creative work is anything that makes meaning for our deepest selves:

> ... creativity means making something for the soul out of every experience. Sometimes we can shape experience into meaningfulness playfully and inventively. At other times, simply holding experience in memory and in reflection allows it to incubate and reveal some of its imagination. ... Creative work can be exciting, inspiring and godlike, but it is also ...

humdrum, and full of anxieties, frustrations, dead ends, mistakes. . . .
Creativity is, foremost, being in the world soulfully, for the only thing we
truly make whether in the arts, in culture, or at home is soul.[1]

We might not be accustomed to considering how to "make something
for our souls" out of the humdrum of our work or from work-related
"frustrations, dead ends, mistakes." But reflect for a moment on your experience of these:

- Has something creative ever come from your own "frustrations, dead
  ends, mistakes"?
- What aspect of your work is particularly humdrum? How might this
  be or become creative or soul-ful?
- Where in your work do you find yourself being most creative?
- What in the wisdom of your spiritual tradition relates to creativity
  in work?

Respond: Broadening our understanding of creativity may open us to
experiencing work in deeper, more meaningful ways. Let's consider how
the insights we've begun to generate today might be applied in our own
work contexts.

- What insights from today's conversation seem especially useful to
  you?
- How might you apply these insights to your own life or work situation?
- What action step would you be willing to undertake in response to
  today's conversation?

Bless: Offer the person on your left a word of blessing or hope for the coming week.

Note

1. Thomas Moore, *Care of the Soul, A Guide for Cultivating Depth and Sacredness in
Everyday Living* (New York: HarperPerennial, 1994) (paperback), 198, 199.

IV: Dealing creatively with failure

Center: Take a deep breath and become aware of any tension in your body. Relax that tension and imagine you are being held in a circle of warm and healing Light. Relax as this Light "melts" the stresses of the day. Rest in the wholeness this Light is bringing you.

Check in: Can you share something of what's currently happening for you at work?

Focus: Failure is an experience common to almost everyone, but our tendency is to regard it simply as negative. Today, however, we explore failure as a work of the soul. A number of years ago, researchers at MIT did a study of failure. They found that there were two types of response to failure. Some people viewed failure as "bad," responding with discouragement and even defeat. Others were somehow energized by failure; though the experience might be painful, they saw it as a chance to learn something new. The researchers called these two attitudes "Failure-Bad" and "Failure-Learn."

- Can you recall a time when you—or someone you know well—experienced some work-related failure? Was it "failure-bad" or "failure-learn?"
- What made the situation either "failure-bad" or "-learn" for those involved?

Reflect: Our attitudes about failure come from somewhere: from our distant past, from our own expectations or sense of ourselves. Reflect for a moment about your past experience with and feelings about failure, exploring privately the roots of your own attitude toward failure. If you wish, jot down any thoughts you want to capture.

- What can you share that might be useful to today's exploration of failure as "soul work"?
- Who taught you the most about failure? How were these lessons creative or less-than-creative in shaping your own attitude toward failure?

Connect: Failure can teach us things about what's important to us, putting us in deeper touch with our soul's vision. In his book *The Fifth Discipline*, Peter Senge suggests that failure "is, simply, a shortfall, evidence of the gap between vision and current reality." He cites a plaque that hung on the wall of Ed Land, the inventor of the Polaroid-Land camera. The plaque read, "A mistake is an event, the full benefit of which has not yet been turned to your advantage."[1]

- What have your own experiences of failure taught you about your deepest values or vision?
- How has failure helped to form or re-form this vision?

Respond: Whether we let failure discourage us or energize us is largely a matter of choice. It can nourish or defeat the soul and, while there may be real and legitimate grief involved, there can also be the seeds of something new.

- Can you envision the "something new" in a recent failure of your own?
- What choices might you make to insure your own failure is "failure-learn"?
- What insights will you take away from today's conversation?

Bless: Offer the person on your left a word of blessing or hope for the coming week.

Note

1. Peter Senge, *The Fifth Discipline: The Art and Practice of the Learning Organization* (Doubleday: New York, 1990), 154.

change: transforming or traumatic?

I: Uncertainty

Center: Take a few deep breaths, letting your body relax more deeply with each exhalation. Become aware that even as you sit here, you are surrounded by divine Mystery. This Mystery holds you and this conversation community in a deep peace that transcends and yet contains all that is in us: all we hope for, all we fear, all we love, all we are. Let yourself rest in this peace and in the Mystery from which it flows, relaxing ever more fully, breathing ever more deeply as you let it fill you and surround you.

Check in: Can you share something about a recent action step? Or, if you prefer, share something for which you've been most—or least—thankful this week.

Focus: Uncertainty seems to be a fact of life in today's workplace and indeed in the culture at large. Today we look at some of the uncertainties we experience in our lives, especially at work, and consider ways we might approach these creatively.

- Where in your own life, especially at work, are you currently experiencing uncertainty?

- How is this experience for you; what feelings, thoughts, imaginings does it evoke in you?
- Can you recall other times of uncertainty in your life? What did you learn from these times?

Reflect: Uncertainty can certainly be uncomfortable, and yet maybe there are ways to "hold" it that invite the emergence of something new or creative. Uncertainty invites the imagination to play. Perhaps what we imagine may be fearful, but might it also lead us to dream or stretch us to envision something heretofore unconsidered? In his book *Soulmaker,* Michael Grosso suggests that "Great dreams contain inexhaustible truths, and orient us, like runes, toward our futures. One hesitates to try to explain them; one wants to dance them, act them out in living gestures. The more we put ourselves into a great dream, the more we get back. Great dreams are wells that never run dry."[1] While Grosso is speaking about the dreams we have when we sleep, his words might apply as well to our daytime hopes and fantasies. Let's take a moment to reflect on the imaginings and dreams—both positive and negative—we create around our own uncertainties.

- What do you notice about your own hoping, imagining, and dreaming?
- How do your fantasies "orient [you] toward [your own] future"?
- What's the role of choice in your dreaming, imagining, and dealing with uncertainty?

Connect/Respond: Responding creatively to uncertainty may require us to develop a deeper trust in ourselves and in the larger Reality in which we have our being. Many of the world's great spiritual traditions encourage such trust. Review the quotations on page 111, noting which ones especially speak to you.

- Do any of these passages spark an insight for you?
- How does it relate to our conversation so far?
- How does it speak to your own current uncertainty, or does it?
- How might you apply the insights of today's conversation?

Bless: Let's offer a word of hope or blessing for the coming week to the person to our left.

Quotations from *World Scripture:* *A Comparative Anthology of Sacred Texts*

Truly do I exist in all beings, but I am most manifest in man. The human heart is my favorite dwelling place.

—*Hinduism.* Srimad Bhagavatam 11.2[2]

Where there is no vision, the people perish.

—*Judaism and Christianity.* Proverbs 29:18[3]

A man of faith, absorbed in faith, his senses controlled, attains knowledge, and, knowledge attained, quickly finds supreme peace. But the ignorant man, who is without faith, goes doubting to destruction. For the doubting self there is neither this world, nor the next, nor joy.

—*Hinduism.* Bhagavad Gita 4:39–40[4]

For truly, I say to you, if you have faith as a grain of mustard seed, you will move this mountain, "Move from here to there," and it will move; and nothing will be impossible to you.

—*Christianity.* Matthew 17:20[5]

Exhausted after all effort, to the Lord's shelter I go,
  Now that to His shelter I have come, say I,
  "Lord, preserve me or ruin me as may please Thee!"
    —*Sikhism.* Adi Granth, Devgandhari, M.4, 527[6]

Notes

1. Michael Grosso, *Soulmaker,* as quoted in http://www.spiritualityhealth.com/newsh/items/soulbooster/item_328.html.
2. Swami Prabhavananda, ed., Srimad Bhagavatum: *The Wisdom of God* (Hollywood: Vedanta, 1943).
3. The Holy Bible, authorized King James Version.
4. Swami Prabhavananda and Christopher Isherwood, trans., *The Song of God: Bhagavad-Gita* (Hollywood: Vedanta, 1943, 1972).
5. The Holy Bible, Revised Standard Version (New York: National Council of the Churches of Christ in the USA, 1946, 1971).
6. Gurbachan Singh Talib, trans., *Sri Guru Granth Sahib,* 4 vols. (Patiala, India: Public Bureau of Punjabi University, Patiala, 1984), 527.

II: *"Be not afraid . . ."*

Center: Take a few deep breaths, letting your body relax more deeply with each exhalation. Become aware that even as you sit here, you are surrounded by divine Mystery. This Mystery holds you and this conversation community in a deep peace that transcends and yet contains all that is in us: all we hope for, all we fear, all we love, all we are. Let yourself rest in this peace and in the Mystery from which it flows, relaxing ever more fully, breathing ever more deeply as you let it fill you and surround you.

Check in: Can you share something about a recent action step? If you prefer, share whatever has been most life-giving and/or life-draining about your workday or week so far.

Focus: Fear of change is something most of us experience from time to time, at work and elsewhere in our lives. Parker Palmer, teacher and author, speaks of "our fear of the natural chaos of life[:] . . . We want to organize and orchestrate things so thoroughly that messiness will never . . . threaten to overwhelm us (for 'messiness' read dissent, innovation, challenge, and change.)"[1]

- What can you say about your own experience with fear at work?
- Are there innovations, challenges, or changes that currently "threaten to overwhelm" you?
- In what sorts of circumstances do you experience discomfort with life's "messiness"?

Reflect: Palmer goes on to suggest that "chaos is the precondition to creativity: as every creation myth has it, life itself emerged from the void."

- Have you ever had an experience of creativity emerging from "chaos"?
- What makes chaos creative rather than, well, just chaotic? What prevents chaos from being creative?

Connect: How are we to deal creatively with fear? Palmer again: ". . . we can remind each other of the dominant role that fear plays in our lives, of all the ways that fear forecloses [our potential.] . . . [A]ll of the world's wisdom traditions address the fact of fear [and] . . . all of them unite in one exhortation . . .: 'Be not afraid.' . . . [This] does not mean we [are not to] *have* fear. Everyone has fear . . . Instead the words say we do not need to *be* the fear we have. We do not have to lead from a place of fear, thereby engendering a world in which fear is multiplied."

- What does it mean that "we do not need to *be* the fear we have"? What's the difference between "being" and "having" fear?
- When we experience fear, can we lead *ourselves* in such a way that our fear isn't multiplied? How?
- What wisdom from your own spiritual tradition helps when you experience fear?

Respond: Let's consider how we're drawn to respond to the insights of today's conversation:
- What insight will you take away from our time together today?
- What action step might you take in response to today's conversation?

Bless: Let's close by offering the person on our left a word of hope or blessing for the coming week.

Note

1. Parker Palmer, *Let Your Life Speak: Listening for the Voice of Vocation* (San Francisco: Jossey-Bass, 2000), 89.

III: *Living faithfully in the midst of layoffs*

Center: Take a few deep breaths, letting your body relax more deeply with each exhalation. Become aware that even as you sit here, you are surrounded by divine Mystery. This Mystery holds you and this conversation community in a deep peace that transcends and yet contains all that is in us: all we hope for, all we fear, all we love, all we are. Let yourself rest in this peace and in the Mystery from which it flows, relaxing ever more fully, breathing ever more deeply as you let it fill you and surround you.

Check in: Can you share something about an action step you're working on at the moment; or if you prefer, share the work-related concern most on your mind at the moment?

Focus: From time to time even the strongest economies experience downturns resulting in layoffs for a number of business communities. When layoffs are announced or are a possibility within a firm, the organization "shudders" as it were, and individuals respond in a variety of ways. Today we look at issues of significant job transition.
- Have you ever been laid off or faced the immanent possibility of a layoff? What was this like for you?
- In your experience, what effect does the threat of layoffs or impending job transition have on the workplace? On your own experience of work?

Reflect: Whether our own jobs are lost or threatened, we may be watching others struggle with this possibility, or perhaps we're the one having to make the layoffs. People of faith want to make a creative response, to find some way to offer leadership in this difficult situation. We may wonder, though, what sort of response is likely to be creative.

- In your own experience, what are some creative ways to face job transition?
- What kinds of things support community within an organization facing layoffs?
- How might an organization—and the individuals within such organization—make layoffs life-giving for those affected and those who remain employed by the organization?

Connect: The question we've been considering might be framed, "What does it mean to live and work faithfully when my organization is making layoffs or I'm having to change jobs?" From the Sufi tradition of Islam come words that may inform our consideration of these questions. Let's look at the passage below.

- What in this selection strikes you as being relevant to our conversation?
- What from your own spiritual tradition is helpful as you consider what it means to be faithful in context of the workplace transition?
- Looking at the five steps involved in "Following the Way," can you imagine how they apply to your current work situation?

Respond: Let's look at ways to "walk" today's "talk":

- What insights will you take away from today's conversation?
- What action steps might you make in response to these insights?
- How might this conversation community support you in these?

Bless: Offer the person on your left a word of hope or blessing for the coming week.

From the Sufi Tradition of Islam[1]:

Following the Way

This is the lesson on following the Way. Remember it.

1. **Go where you are sent.**
   Going where I am sent means following my love.

2. **Wait until you are shown what to do.**
   Waiting is an act, a decision to be present at the birth of what-is-not-yet.
3. **Do it with your whole self.**
   When the fragmented self is fused together by the heat of love, it shows its wholeness in: vulnerability, authority, and passion.
4. **Remain until you have done what you were sent to do.**
   Learn to read the changes in yourself, in the thing itself, in the face of God.
5. **Walk away with empty hands.**
   Those who go with God must travel as God travels: trusting the journey's end.

No one will ever tell you that the Way is easy: only that it is possible.

No one can tell you if the journey is worthwhile, for your wages are concealed in the hand of God, and will be shown you only on the last day of eternity.

But whoever chooses to follow the Way will have the joyous company of God's beloved fools as fellow travelers, and a resting place, at journey's end, in the Mecca of the heart.

Note

1. These notes are taken from materials prepared by the Rev. M. R. Ritley, an Episcopal priest and Sufi master, currently serving at the Church of the Good Shepherd in Berkeley, CA. Used by permission.

IV: *What's not wrong—The power of choice*

Center: Take a few deep breaths, letting your body relax more deeply with each exhalation. Become aware that even as you sit here, you are surrounded by divine Mystery. This Mystery holds you and this conversation community in a deep peace that transcends and yet contains all that is in us: all we hope for, all we fear, all we love, all we are. Let yourself rest in this peace and in the Mystery from which it flows, relaxing ever more fully, breathing ever more deeply as you let it fill you and surround you.

Check in: If you wish, share something of your centering meditation; or something of what you're most or least grateful for.

Focus/Reflect: Most of us will have heard the metaphor expressing the power of choice captured in the question: "Is your cup half-full or half-empty?" Often, however, our attitudes and choices about work are not fully conscious. Dealing creatively with change in our work lives may necessitate our becoming more aware of our attitudes, and making conscious choices about how we will regard our work.

- Can you share a personal anecdote that captures the meaning of either "half-full" or "half-empty"?
- Is there a situation at work right now that you've been seeing as "half-empty" (or completely empty!)?
- What would it take to transform the "half-empty" into "half-full"?

Connect: In his book of reflections *Peace Is Every Step: The Path of Mindfulness in Everyday Life,* Buddhist monk Thich Nhat Hanh wonders why we so often dwell on what's wrong in our lives rather than asking the question, "What's not wrong?" His short meditation is on the next page.

- Can you think of an occasion in your own life when you asked, "What's wrong?" when you might have asked, "What's *not* wrong?"
- What aspect of your own work life that you're taking for granted might you enjoy actively, in the way that Thich Nhat Hahn appreciates his breathing?
- Are there spiritual disciplines from your own faith tradition that you employ to help yourself become more mindful, practices that shift your "seeing" from half-empty to half-full?
- When might it be important to see and respond to the "what's wrongs" in our lives?
- What is the difference between mind*ful*ness that focuses on the positive and mind*less*ness that represses anything uncomfortable?

Respond: Let's consider how we might respond in the coming week to the insights of today's conversation. Here are a few ideas to get us thinking; could you:

1. Leave a coffee cup half full of water on your desk, or create some other visual reminder of today's conversation?
2. Express appreciation to co-workers to whom you might recently have complained?
3. Reflect more deeply on the "what's wrongs" of your work situation, sorting out those which need creative attention and resolution and those which can be re-envisioned in a more hopeful light?
4. Make the choice to pay more appreciative attention to some small aspect of your life you've taken for granted?
5. Take more notice of the creative aspects of your work environment that you tend to overlook: plants growing in entrance halls, the sky from your office window, the humanity of the security personnel, etc.?

Is there one of these or another action step you'd be willing to try this week?

Bless: As we close, offer the person on your left a simple word of hope or blessing for the coming week.

"What's Not Wrong?"[1] by Thich Nhat Hanh

We often ask, "What's wrong?" Doing so, we invite painful seeds of sorrow to come up and manifest. We feel suffering, anger, and depression, and produce more such seeds. We would be much happier if we tried to stay in touch with the healthy, joyful seeds inside of us and around us. We should learn to ask, "What's not wrong?" and be in touch with that. There are so many elements in the world and within our bodies, feelings, perceptions, and consciousness that are wholesome, refreshing, and healing. If we block ourselves, if we stay in the prison of our sorrow, we will not be in touch with these healing elements.

Life is filled with many wonders, like the blue sky, the sunshine, the eyes of a baby. Our breathing, for example, can be very enjoyable. I enjoy breathing everyday. But many people appreciate the joy of breathing only when they have asthma or a stuffed-up nose. We don't need to wait until we have asthma to enjoy our breathing. Awareness of the precious elements of happiness is itself the practice of right mindfulness. Elements like these are within us and all around us. In each second of our lives we can enjoy them. If we do so, seeds of peace, joy, and happiness will be planted in us, and they will become strong. The secret to happiness is happiness itself. Wherever we are, any time, we have the capacity to enjoy the sunshine, the presence of each other, the wonder of our breathings. We don't have to travel anywhere else to do so. We can be in touch with these things right now.

Take a moment now to enjoy your own breathing. Breathe deeply and slowly, letting yourself feel the breath enter every corner of your lungs. Then letting the breath go, relax as you feel it leave your lungs until you have to push the remaining air out. Breathe mindfully in this way for a minute or so.

Note

1. Thich Nhat Hanh, *Peace Is Every Step: The Path of Mindfulness in Everyday Life* (New York: Bantum Books, 1992), 77–78.

holiday issues in the workplace

I: What are they, and how do we address them?

Center: Imagine a favorite place or time when you felt real peace and quiet joy. Take a moment to center yourself, returning to that time or place. Feel its serenity. Let yourself relax into its safety. Become aware of the presence of divine Mystery around you. Let the peace of that time and place flow into your body, continuing to reside there as you return to this time and place.

Check in: Can you share something about the action step you've been working on? If you prefer, share a work-related high or low point of your week so far.

Focus: Holiday times are a curious combination of anticipation and stress, joy and frustration. For many they can be a time of loneliness or heart-aching nostalgia, as well. The workplace can both add to this tension and be a locus in which the tension is manifested. But can it be anything else? As we often do, let's begin with our own experience:

- Do you have an anecdote, memory, or image that captures for you the tension of this holiday season?

- What's happening at your own workplace that reminds you of the ways holiday times are a mixed blessing?
- What work-related or personal issues surface for you or those you know at this time of year?

Reflect/Connect: The spiritual wisdom of most traditions counsels a kind of balance we don't often see in ourselves or others at this time of year. Chances are, however, that most of us can remember a moment in holidays past when we *did* get in touch with something deeper, the something deeper toward which the holidays are meant to point. Reflect for a minute on when this moment—whether fleeting or prolonged—might have been for you.

- Can you recall what about the context of the situation, whether it was an external or internal context, facilitated your connecting with deeper meaning?
- How does your own spiritual tradition assist you to maintain balance during the holidays?
- Are there spiritual readings, practices, or rituals that deepen your wholeness during this special time?
- Are there ways in which the spiritual insights you've collected from past holidays might assist you and others in dealing with holiday concerns that surface in the workplace this time of year?

Respond: The pressures of the holiday season sometimes make it imperative that we make a conscious choice to seek life-giving alternatives. We might decide, for example, to:

1. Identify one holiday pattern that has tended to be life-draining in the past and make a change this year.
2. Conduct an informal conversation with a few work colleagues to discover whether they might like changes made in work-related holiday tasks.
3. Choose a prayer or meditative technique to which you've felt yourself drawn, and practice it faithfully for a period of time that seems manageable for you.
4. Find a poem, wisdom saying, or other meaningful phrase that reminds you to maintain a balance; place it on your desk or share it with a friend at work.

Is there one of these actions you'd be willing to experiment with this week? How else might you apply the insights of today's conversation to your work life?

Bless: Offer the person on your left a word of blessing or hope for this holiday season.

II: Can we "make spirits bright" at work?

Center: Imagine a favorite place or time when you felt real peace and quiet joy. Take a moment to center yourself, returning to that time or place. Feel its serenity. Let yourself relax into its safety. Become aware of the presence of divine Mystery around you. Let the peace of that time and place flow into your body, continuing to reside there as you return to this time and place.

Check in: Can you share something about the action step you chose as a result of the last conversation? If you prefer, share whatever you are most and/or least thankful for at work right now.

Focus: The holiday season is a time of paradox in the workplace, a time of promise and frustration when a genuine desire for connection sometimes competes with a sort of "holiday correctness." There are those we truly enjoy honoring with a card or gift and those we may feel obligated to remember. There are folks with whom we look forward to spending time and parties that command our attendance. Let's see what we can make of our experience of workplace holidays.

- Can you recall a workplace holiday moment that was especially meaningful to you?
- Can you recall a workplace holiday event or moment that seemed a waste of time?
- What is the purpose, the expected outcome, of the holiday celebrations at work? In what ways do these events fulfill or fall short of these outcomes?
- In what ways does the holiday theme of "making spirits bright" seem to fit your workplace? In what ways does it feel incongruous? Can you express this congruence/incongruence in an image?
- If you could design the ideal workplace holiday celebration, what would it include?

Reflect/Connect: The wisdom of many spiritual traditions recognizes the importance of right action. The core of the Judeo/Christian tradition, for example, is sometimes expressed in the exhortation to love God with your whole being and your neighbor as yourself. The holiday season, ironically, may actually pose a challenge to our incarnating this wisdom in a meaningful way, a challenge to a deeper sort of "making spirits bright."

- How would you describe your own deepest needs during the holidays?
- What have you noticed about the spiritual needs of your neighbors at work during this time?
- What might "loving God and your neighbor as yourself" mean in your workplace right now?

Respond: It is rarely possible to fulfill all the needs we recognize in ourselves or others, whether at this or any time of the year. Sometimes however, there are ways to "meet" needs, that is, to acknowledge and hence honor them, even though we can't, strictly speaking, fulfill them. Here are some ways we might do this:

1. Spend a quiet moment with yourself, and list the gifts, spiritual, emotional, and, yes, material, you'd really like to receive this year. Pause over those you know will not be given and let yourself "grieve" their "loss."
2. Reflect on the needs of your closest colleagues, and find some small ways to acknowledge them whenever it's possible.
3. Choose a prayer or meditative technique to which you've felt drawn, and practice it faithfully for a period of time that seems manageable for you.
4. Write a letter to yourself listing a few things you'd like to do for someone else once the hoopla of the season is over; give it to your secretary or a friend to mail to you in a few weeks or months.

Is there one of these actions you'd be willing to experiment with this week? How else might you apply the insights of today's conversation to your work life?

Bless: Offer the person on your left a word of blessing or hope for this holiday season.

III: *Making meaning of the New Year transition*

Center: Let yourself relax, breathing deeply and opening to the One who is greater than you, let the peace of that One fill you. Recall for a moment the year now coming to a close. Recall the significant moments of your work life: the highs, the lows. Breathe deeply as you remember, and again, let the peace of the Divine fill you as you relax into that peace. Continue your review of the year. Give silent thanks for what went well and gently let go for now of anything troubling. Once again, relax into the peace of divine Mystery.

Check in: Can you share something about the action step you chose as a result of the last conversation? If you prefer, share whatever work-related concern is on your mind.

Focus: In our culture the New Year acts as a sort of culturally induced transition: we reflect on the past year and look ahead with hope to the coming year. Inevitably, too, we fit the past year into the tapestry of years lived, looking for patterns, for meaning. Let's begin with memories and reflections on the past year. If you wish, list the significant work-related events—personal or communal, positive or negative—of your past year.
   - What was the highlight of your year at work?
   - Can you recall a significant work-related insight or learning from the past year?
   - What work-related transitions occurred for you in the year just past?

Reflect: Only a few of us take our New Year's resolutions with great seriousness, but the practice of making them does afford us the opportunity to recall what we most value and to re-orient ourselves toward these values.
   - Can you recall any of the resolutions you made last year? Did any have real significance for you? Any from years past?
   - If you could make a New Year's resolution for your workplace or professional community, what would it be?
   - What is your deepest hope for your own work in the New Year?

Connect: New Year's resolutions, as well as our memories of the past and our hopes for the future, give us useful clues about our own souls: what's important to them and how we can best honor them.
   - How does what you remember of the past year—either positive or painful memories—help you understand what's most important to you?
   - What values underlie your New Year's resolutions from years past or for the coming year?
   - What patterns do you notice about your New Year's reflections or resolutions? Are there any common themes that seem to resurface year after year?

Respond: The New Year can be an occasion for becoming more intentional about practicing our values. Can you formulate an action step—a work-related New Year's resolution—related to one of the values we've just discussed? Here are some other action steps you might consider:

1. Explore the values that underlie your memories and hopes. Make one decision about honoring one or more of these values.
2. Make a list of twelve small, do-able, work-related "resolutions of the month," and post it where you'll see it often.
3. Make several "relationship resolutions" regarding any relational issues in your workplace.
4. Select a general category (e.g., spiritual growth, physical fitness, etc.) and meditate over several days on how you might honor yourself in this area. From this meditation, generate action steps.

What action step will you take as a result of today's conversation?

Bless: Offer the person on your left a word of hope or blessing for the New Year.

IV: Workplace "resolutions" for the New Year

Center: Reflect for a moment on your morning: imagine yourself before work. Perhaps you were on public transit or in your car. Perhaps you were having a cup of tea or coffee. Picture yourself as you were, but become aware of the Divine with you. Now picture yourself entering your workspace: Divine Mystery is already there, awaiting your arrival. Imagine this Mystery present during the various activities and encounters of your morning. Now become aware of the Divine with us now.

Check in: Can you share something about the action step you chose as a result of the last conversation? If you prefer, share a work-related concern, thought, or need.

Focus: We hear a lot of talk this time of year about New Year's resolutions; we may feel a bit jaded about such resolutions. The word *resolution,* though, has a great many meanings. What if we interpreted *New Year's resolutions* as "the successful conclusion or completion of . . ."? Reflect silently for a moment on the various levels of your own life, especially perhaps your work life, naming for yourself some issues, conflicts, situations, or relationships for which you hope for resolution, a "successful completion," in the coming months. These levels may include:

- ✔ Your individual work
- ✔ The work group of which you are a part
- ✔ The larger corporation/institution that "contains" you and your colleagues
- ✔ The profession, field, or business community of which your organization is a part
- ✔ The wider society in which we all find places

■ Can you share one situation or conflict that came to mind as you reflected?

■ What image or metaphor expresses the situation that came to your mind? What image or metaphor might express the resolution you hope for?

Reflect: Another meaning of *resolution,* according the Webster's Collegiate, is "the act or process of reducing to a simpler form." Consider the situations, conflicts, or relationships we've just been discussing:

■ What might "reducing to a simpler form" mean for you in one or more of these situations?

■ Are there other issues or complexities in your work life, personal or corporate, that seem to beg for such reduction, that is, beg for resolution?

Connect/Respond: On page 126 is a quotation from a contemporary paraphrase of the *Tao Te Ching.* Let's see whether its wisdom throws any light on our hoped-for resolutions.

■ How does this excerpt speak to your own situation/experience?

■ What insights occur to you as you read this passage?

■ Are there helpful images or sayings from your own spiritual tradition that might inform our conversation?

■ What might be your own part in the "New Year's resolution" of whatever workplace situation, conflict, or relationship came to your mind during today's conversation? What is the first step you might take in acting toward this "resolution"?

Bless: Offer the person on your left a word of hope or blessing for the New Year.

From John Heider's
The Tao of Leadership: Lao Tzu's Tao Te Ching Adapted for a New Age[1]

14: Knowing What Is Happening

When you cannot see what is happening in a group, do not stare harder. Relax and look gently with your inner eye.

When you do not understand what a person is saying, do not grasp for every word. Give up your efforts. Become silent inside and listen with your deepest self.

When you are puzzled by what you see or hear, do not strive to figure things out. Stand back for a moment and be calm. When a person is calm, complex events appear simple.

To know what is happening, push less, open out and be aware. See without staring. Listen quietly rather than listening hard. Use intuition and reflections rather than trying to figure things out.

The more you can let go of trying, and the more open and receptive you become, the more easily you will know what is happening.

Also, stay in the present. The present is more available than either memories of the past or fantasies of the future.

So attend to what is happening now.

Note

1. John Heider, *The Tao of Leadership: Lao Tzu's Tao Te Ching Adapted for a New Age* (Atlanta: Humanics New Age, 1985), 27.

part III:
other conversation formats for spirituality at work groups

introduction

The formats that follow are ones with which we've had some experience and that we've found to be useful to participants. For each of these, we've summarized how the model works in our experience. In addition, at the beginning of each summary we've tried to say what we've learned regarding:

Time: The optimum time needed for a good conversation using the given format.

Group composition: Whether the format works best with a fixed membership (i.e., is closed to additional participants once the composition is fixed) or works fine with membership that varies and is open to additional participants.

Leadership: The type of leadership that works for the given model, whether some sort of training or experience is useful, and whether shared leadership (i.e., leadership rotated among participants) is advisable.

Attendance: The attendance norms appropriate for each conversation model (i.e., is regular attendance essential or is occasional attendance by participants sufficient?).

Methodology: A step-by-step walk-through of the process involved in the given format. Some of the formats rely heavily on the work of others; where this is so, we've cited the work on which our format is based.

transformative storytelling[1]

Time: About 1 hour.

Group composition: Usually fixed.

Leadership: Presenter and facilitator, but leadership can rotate. Some experience with model useful for leaders.

Attendance: Regular is best.

Methodology: One person, the presenter, prepares a brief story of an incident that occurred at work. It can be an encounter with another person, a "moral dilemma" of some sort, an ongoing office dynamic, whatever. It is useful to write this up ahead of time. The crucial thing is that the story be thought out fairly carefully because the time for the storytelling is short. A second person, the facilitator, takes responsibility for making sure the wisdom of all participants is brought to bear on the story presented and for moving the group through the several reflection steps.

Here's the way the process itself works.

Step 1: Storytelling (5 min.)

Presenter reads his/her story aloud. One of the reasons it's useful to write the story out ahead of time is that such preparation insures the story will be succinct (two single-spaced pages = 5 minutes).

Step 2: Understanding the story (5 min.)

Participants ask clarifying questions of the presenter about his/her story but at this point *offer no comment,* analysis, or advice. The idea is to be sure that everyone understands what's happening and any relevant background information.

Step 3: Sharing personal wisdom (10 min.)

Participants share briefly the personal connections—memories, feelings, images, etc.—between the presenter's story and their own lived experience *while the presenter listens.* This is not yet the time for participants to give advice or problem solve; rather, they just tell something of their own stories that relate to the focus story.

   (Note: It's often hard for the presenter just to listen and for the participants not to expect a response from the presenter; nevertheless, the effectiveness of the format depends on this. The presenter may, however, find it useful to take notes during the times when he/she is listening.)

Step 4: Sharing professional wisdom (10 min.)

Participants share briefly any insights they may have based on their own professional wisdom or training. This is a chance to hear diverse perspectives based on the participants' varied work or educational backgrounds. Again, the *presenter listens* to these "professional stories" without comment or reaction.

Step 5: Spiritual reflection (10 min.)

Participants share and discuss stories, images, and insights from their own *spiritual* tradition that come to their minds as they reflect on the case. This part of the discussion helps the group relate spirituality to the real-life situation presented. Again, the *presenter listens without comment or reaction.*

Step 6: Reflection on action (10 min.)

Participants reflect on the effectiveness of whatever action the presenter has already taken and suggest possible future action steps. Now is the time for advice and problem solving, to which the *presenter still simply listens.*

Step 7: Presenter response and evaluation (5 min.)

Presenter is now asked by the facilitator to share his/her learnings and response to what has been said.

General comments: Transformative Storytelling can be used on an "as needed" basis with any ongoing spirituality at work conversation. However, when used regularly, it is an excellent process for a group that is serious about integrating spirituality and work. In such a conversation community, commitment to the group and to regular attendance would be rather important, although the group might not meet as frequently as other types of groups. Generally, too, the composition for this sort of group would be fixed, with newcomers invited by agreement of the whole group or at designated intervals.

The storytelling process itself takes only an hour, especially when the presenter is well prepared. If check-in and/or prayer are a regular part of the group's time, however, an extra 15 or 20 minutes is needed.

Note

1. Based on *Shared Wisdom: A Guide to Case Study Reflection in Ministry* by J. H. Mahan, B. B. Troxell, and C. J. Allen (Nashville: Abington, 1993).

contemplative "conversation"[1]

Time: 1 to 1$^1/_2$ hours.

Group composition: Fixed is best.

Leadership: Convenor is useful. Shared leadership works well. No training needed.

Attendance: Regular is best.

Methodology: This methodology is entirely contemplative; there is sharing, but no conversation in the usual sense. The convenor manages the time, moving the group to the next step when appropriate.

Step 1: Check-in (5 min.)

Check-in consists of one or two words describing your feeling state (i.e., anxious, mellow, revved up, etc.). To do this format in an hour, the convenor must start the group promptly and limit check-in. (Latecomers can slip in quietly after the group has begun.) If time permits, a longer check-in is possible.

Step 2: Individual reflection (10 min.)

Participants reflect silently on the question: "Where have I encountered divine Mystery at work in the past week?" The group may stay together in a circle, or if time permits, participants can leave the circle to find a private spot.

Step 3: Communal reflection (10 min.)

The convenor invites participants to reflect aloud on their time of private reflection. They do not comment on each other's reflections. Since this is a contemplative model, frequent periods of silence occur even during the times of communal reflection. The silences provide an opportunity to listen for the Mystery; the speaking/sharing becomes richer when it emerges from this silent listening.

Step 4: Individual reflection (15 min.)

Participants return to individual prayer, again leaving the circle if time permits. This time, the focus is on divine Presence in the whole of one's work life: past, present, and future. Aware that Spirit is with them in the present moment, participants hold their lives—joys, anxieties, hurts, thanksgivings, angers—before the Divine.

Step 5: Communal reflection (10 min.)

The convenor asks the question "Where did you meet the Divine in this reflection time?" and again invites the group to reflect aloud on their time of private reflection. As before, participants share contemplatively without commenting on each other's reflections.

Step 6: Discerning a theme (5 min.)

The convenor asks, "Does anyone see a theme?" One or two participants offer comments about any theme that may have emerged from the communal reflection time.

Step 7: Closing word (5 min.)

The convenor calls the group to a close by inviting participants to describe in a word or two where they are now and how they feel as they prepare to leave the group.

General comments: This format is most fruitful when participants are committed to regular attendance and the community is allowed to develop as time goes on. Groups who have used this model say that even though there is no conversation, powerful themes emerge that deepen over time, and genuine transformation occurs both within the lives of individuals and the life of the community. This model also assumes that individuals are praying regularly or meditating on their own.

Note

1. Based on the Friends of the Mystery model developed by Br. Jack Mostyn, Congregation of Christian Brothers, 33 Pryer Terrace, New Rochelle, New York. Used with permission.

spirituality at work book group

Time: 1 hour.

Group composition: Fixed.

Leadership: Convenor prepares beforehand. Shared leadership works well with no training needed.

Attendance: Regular is best.

Methodology: Prior to the meeting, the group or convenor selects a book to read. Especially recommended are books relating spirituality and work, but almost anything that interests the group can be used (see possible titles below). The convenor reads the material ahead of time (usually a chapter) and selects passages or paragraphs to be read aloud. If time permits, s/he also prepares focus questions (see Step Three below).

Step 1: Gathering/check-in (15 min.)

Participants share how their day is going so far or anything else that is noteworthy in their lives.

Step 2: Communal reading (10 min.)

Convenor reads aloud the selected excerpts from the book, or asks others to do so. (These passages can be marked out in order to facilitate another's reading them.) If desired, the convenor can summarize points not covered in the passages read aloud. The convenor may ask the group to focus on something that will ready them for the conversation to follow (e.g., ask the group to "listen for questions" they may have as the passage is read, or to see what images come to mind during the reading).

Step 3: Conversation (20 min.)

The convenor facilitates conversation around the reading, focusing the conversation by:
- Asking the group to share the questions that occurred to them during the reading or
- Inviting the group to share any memories or anecdotes the passage may have evoked in them or
- Asking if the passage speaks to any situation they're dealing with at work or
- Suggesting the group share any images or feelings prompted by the reading or
- Inviting participants to share something from the wisdom of their own spiritual tradition that came to mind during the reading.

Step 4: Respond (10 min.)

Convenor suggests the group reflect on the practical application the passage might have for their own work context and invites participants to decide what action steps they will take in response to this reflection.

Step 5: Closing (5 min.)

Group closes with prayer or a word of hope.

Suggested Resources for Book Groups

Banks, Robert J. , ed. *Faith Goes to Work: Reflections from the Marketplace.* Herndon, Va.: Alban Institute, 1993.

Brussat, Frederic and Mary Ann. *Spiritual Literacy: Reading the Sacred in Everyday Life.* New York: Scribner, 1996.

Canfield, Jack, Mark Victor Hansen, Maida Rogerson, Martin Rutte, and Tim Clauss. *Chicken Soup for the Soul at Work.* Deerfield Beach, Fla.: Health Communications, 1996.

Carlson, Richard. *Don't Sweat the Small Stuff: Simple Ways to Keep the Little Things from Taking over Your Life.* New York: Hyperion, 1997.

Diehl, William. *The Monday Connection: A Spirituality of Competence, Affirmation, and Support in the Workplace.* New York: HarperCollins, 1991.

————. *Ministry in Daily Life: A Practical Guide for Congregations.* Herndon, Va.: Alban Institute, 1996.

Fox, Matthew. *The Reinvention of Work: A New Vision of Livelihood for Our Time.* New York: HarperSanFrancisco, 1994.

Heider, John. *The Tao of Leadership.* Atlanta: Humanic New Age, 1985.

Krueger, David A. *Keeping Faith at Work: The Christian in the Workplace.* Nashville: Abington Press, 1994.

Needleman, Jacob. *Money and the Meaning of Life.* New York: Doubleday, 1991.

Palmer, Parker. *The Active Life: Wisdom for Work, Creativity and Caring.* New York: HarperSanFrancisco, 1991.

————. *Let Your Life Speak.* San Francisco: Jossey-Bass, 2000.

Remen, Rachel Naomi. *Kitchen Table Wisdom: Stories that Heal.* New York: Riverhead Books, 1996.

Richmond, Lewis. *Work as a Spiritual Discipline: A Practical Buddhist Approach to Inner Growth and Satisfaction on the Job.* New York: Broadway Book, 1999.

Salkin, Jeffrey K. *Being God's Partner: How to Find the Hidden Link Between Spirituality and Your Work.* Woodstock, Vt.: Jewish Lights Publishing, 1994.

Wheatly, Meg, with Myron Kellner-Rogers. *A Simpler Way.* San Francisco: Berrett-Koehler, 1996.

collaborative
inquiry group

Time: Varies with group.

Group composition: Fixed is best after initial meetings.

Leadership: Facilitator is useful, especially initially. Experience with participatory leadership is also useful.

Attendance: Regular is best.

Methodology: The following describes phases in an ongoing inquiry conversation rather than steps in a single session. The format used in a single session would depend on the length of the session, which is determined by the group. Generally, the group builds its agenda at the start of each meeting.

Phase 1: Initiation

One or two people interested in exploring a certain issue related to their experience of spirituality and work invite others to explore the possibility of doing an inquiry group. One or two initial meetings gather interested persons to discuss the topic and inquiry process. Possible topics might be: creating community at work, meeting divine Mystery in/through/ at work, managing the company's ethics, etc. These initial sessions are strictly exploratory; attendance does not imply a commitment to the inquiry group.

Phase 2: Beginning the inquiry—first reflection phase

The first meeting of those who *do* decide to commit to the inquiry is necessarily a longer one; in some cases, two or more setup meetings will be necessary. Three tasks comprise this start-up process:

1. **Generating an inquiry question:** Participants meet to focus their area of exploration by formulating an inquiry question. This question should be one in which all participants have a passionate interest; it is this passion that motivates the participants. The inquiry proceeds because those involved genuinely want to discover the answer to their question. (See the General Comments section on page 146 for examples of inquiry questions.)
2. **Contracting:** The group decides how often it will meet and how long each meeting will be. It may also decide the limits of the inquiry itself (total number of meetings), or it may elect to leave this open, agreeing to negotiate the length of the inquiry after it has progressed a bit and the group has a better idea of how long it will need to bring the inquiry to a satisfactory conclusion.
3. **Generating action steps:** In preparation for returning to their work contexts, participants discuss the first steps they need to take to begin answering their inquiry question. Often this involves a more mindful observation of these contexts in light of the question.

Generating the inquiry question and determining appropriate first action steps represent the first reflection phase of the inquiry.

Phase 3: Action phase

Co-inquirers return to their individual work contexts and begin their agreed-upon observations and actions. Most inquiry participants find it useful (even essential) to jot down their observations in a learning journal. The learning journal serves both to record the insights/musings that occur during this action phase and to help maintain the inquiry focus— a way of staying mindful. The communal reflection and the action phases form one reflection-action cycle in the collaborative inquiry.

Phase 4: Subsequent reflection-action cycles

Subsequent reflection meetings: Participants' observations are shared at the next meeting. The group reflects together on the effectiveness of the actions they have taken and the meaning of what they have experienced in relationship to their inquiry question. They ask such questions as: What have we learned? How have our experiences and the actions we have taken furthered our inquiry? What can we do next that will move us closer to answering our question? Through this reflection process, observations become new knowledge from which, in turn, new action steps are generated in preparation for the next action phase of the cycle.

Subsequent action phases: Co-inquirers continue to experiment with each new set of action steps conceived during the group's reflection meetings.

The number of reflection-action cycles varies depending on the needs and goals of the inquiry group.

Phase 5: Communication/conclusion of the inquiry

Groups often discover they want to find a way to communicate the results of their inquiry with others, and this communication phase may be the conclusion of the inquiry. Like the rest of the process, a suitable way for communicating the group's knowledge is determined collaboratively. Some groups write articles for workplace newsletters; some offer workshops that teach either the inquiry process or the results of their own inquiry; some initiate collaborative inquiries with co-workers within their own contexts. In any case, it is important for the group to find a way to celebrate its work together and bring closure to the inquiry.

General comments: Collaborative inquiry is a highly generative process for those most committed to changing the workplace. The model is transformative because the action steps taken can actually influence and transform work and the work environment. The model is highly flexible in terms of length of time required, as the inquiry question can deal with large or small issues. Examples of inquiry questions include: "How can I create a sense of community in my workplace?" "What can I do to decrease the stress level of my work team?" "How can I make my organization more sensitive to the needs of employees with families?" The inquiry can extend a few days or many months; the only requirement is that enough time pass between reflection meetings that participants have a chance to take their agreed-upon action steps. Reflection meetings can vary in length and frequency from an hour weekly to a weekend retreat twice a year depending on the scheduling needs of the participants and the nature of the inquiry. A fairly high degree of commitment to the group and to the inquiry itself is required, however, since 1) the "data" of the inquiry is the experience of the participants and 2) the knowledge is created communally by the entire group. Groups sometimes find that supplementing their own action-reflections cycles with inquiry-related reading is generative.

For more information about collaborative or cooperative inquiry, see *Collaborative Inquiry as a Strategy for Adult Learning,* edited by Lyle Yorks and Elizabeth Kasl (Jossey-Bass, San Francisco, 2002) or *Collaborative Inquiry in Practice* by John Bray, Joyce Lee, Linda Smith, and Lyle Yorks, edited by Peter Reason (Thousand Oaks, Ca.: Sage, 2000).

discerning god's presence at work[1]

Time: 1 hour.

Group composition: Open.

Leadership: Convenor, some facilitation. Shared leadership works well. No training needed.

Attendance: Periodic is acceptable.

Methodology: This format can be used as the basic process of a group or used in combination with other formats. It can also be shortened and used as the group's check-in as part of another format. The convenor needs to manage the time carefully and must be willing to remind the group of time constraints where these exist.

Step 1: Agenda planning (5 min.)

The facilitator for the session asks who would like extra time on the group's agenda. Participants estimate how much time they will need, and the remaining time is allotted equally to the others. If no one needs extra time, the time is divided among the number of participants. The facilitator manages the time and the group process.

Step 2: Group check-in/sharing

Those who do not need extra time check in first, answering these questions:
- ✔ What about my work this week (or today) has been most life-giving?
- ✔ What about my work has been most life-draining?

If several members of the group have requested extra time, one of these questions may be eliminated for the other participants. The convenor manages the time so that all have a chance at least to check in and those who need more time have it.

Step 3: Discernment

For those who have requested more time or, when possible, for the whole group, a third question follows the first two:
- ✔ To what might be God calling me in this situation?

The convenor may facilitate this process, bringing the group into the discussion of this question after the participant has commented.

General Comments
The three questions are based on the *Ignatian Examen,* and the first two can be rephrased in several ways:
- ✔ When did I feel the most/least love this week/today?
- ✔ For what was I most/least grateful?
- ✔ What were my high/low points?
- ✔ When was I happiest/saddest?
- ✔ When did I feel most/least alive?
- ✔ What would I most/least like to re-live?

Note

1. Inspired by a process described in *Sleeping with Bread: Holding What Gives You Life,* by Dennis Linn, Sheila Fabricant Linn, and Matthew Linn, Mahwah, N.J.: Paulist Press, 1995.

permissions

Every effort has been made to trace the copyright owners of material included in this book. The author and publishers would be grateful if any omissions or inaccuracies in these acknowledgements could be brought to their attention for correction in any future edition. They are grateful to the following copyright holders:

Excerpts from *The Tao of Leadership: Lao Tzu's Tao Te Ching Adapted for a New Age* by John Heider, copyright © 1985 by John Heider. Used with permission of Humanics Publishing Group, 12 S. Dixie Hwy., Ste. 200, Lake Worth, FL 33460. *www.humanicspub.com*

"Consecrating the Ordinary," from *Kitchen Table Wisdom* by Rachel Naomi Remen, M.D., copyright © 1996 by Rachel Naomi Remen, M.D. Used by permission of Riverhead Books, an imprint of Penguin Group (USA) Inc.

Excerpt from *Secular Sanctity* by Edward Hays, copyright © 1984 by Edward Hays, Forest of Peace Publishing, 251 Muncie Road, Leavenworth, KS 66048. Used by permission of Forest of Peace Publishing/Ave Maria Press, P.O. Box 428, Notre Dame, IN 46556. *www.avemariapress.com*

Excerpt from *Breakthrough: Meister Eckhart's Creation of Spritiuality in New Translation* by Matthew Fox, copyright © 1980 by Matthew Fox. Used by permis-